Bon Appetit from
my kitchen to yours.

Carol Lee Karlin

Why a second printing? The 1st printing is sold out and with many unfilled orders and no books available anywhere — What was I to do?

So despite the worried voices from my husband Bob & my printer Terry — "What are you going to do with 2,500 more books"?

My reply was that I need the book because it is now part of me and one of the ways that I can share and give to others.

The 2nd printing is the same popular well-tested recipes except many have been freshened up with new ideas and updated information. You'll notice all the personal & friends comments as well.

I also gained valuable insight into food preparation from my TV show "Today's Kitchen". For over 2½ years and 130 shows I had the experience of cooking most of the book's recipes on camera. This provided new challenges in the presentation and timing of the various dishes.
   — I found out that souffles fall on camera just like they do at home.

Hope you enjoy the "freshened" up printing of Karlin's Kitchen
        Again
   Bon Appétit   Carol Lee Karlin

THE BEST FROM
KARLIN'S KITCHEN

BY
CAROL LEE KARLIN

PHOTOGRAPHY BY TIM MORRISSEY
ILLUSTRATED BY YOLANDA HERNANDEZ
DESIGNED BY TRU LINCOLN

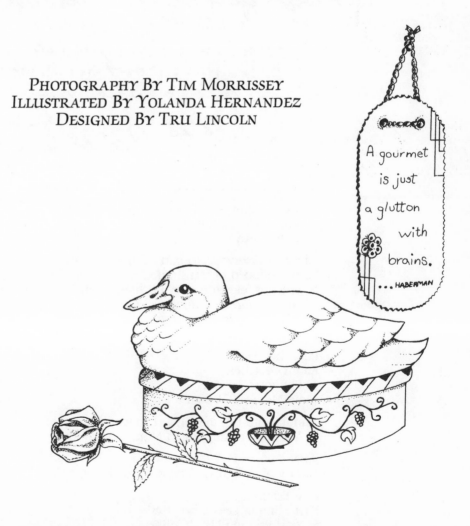

A gourmet is just a glutton with brains.
...HABERMAN

KARLIN'S KITCHEN/PUBLISHER, CALIFORNIA

DEDICATION

Dad—so sorry you didn't get to see this finished. We've sure missed you!

To my Father, *Robert Lee Gill,* who in spite of his struggle with years of blindness provided me the opportunity to complete six years of college and insisted I get my teaching credential.

To my Mother, *Georgia Gill* of Laguna Beach, California who was the first Home Economist in the family and because her role model at home inspired me to pursue the same profession.

Mom—you've been through so much these past few years but what a joy you continue to be in all of our lives.
Love Carol Lee

Text Copyright ©1985 by Carol Lee Karlin
Photography Copyright ©1985 by
Tim Morrissey

Published by
Karlin's Kitchen
1343 Sunset Avenue
Santa Monica, CA 90405

Manufactured in the United States of America by Vaughn Printing, Santa Monica, California.

ISBN 0-9615941-0-1
Library of Congress Catalog Card No. 90-133636

First Edition
First Printing December 1985
Second Printing March 1990

Thanks to all my family, friends & students for using, enjoying and making the 1st printing such a success.

SPECIAL THANKS TO

My husband Bob for paying for the book and putting up with me during all the years of the production.

Ann's Flower's, Santa Monica, California for the lovely centerpiece in the back cover photo.

My student Helene Greenwood for the long months of word-processing the recipes just out of the goodness of her heart.

Janette Miller, my neighbor, who typed and proof-read for weeks to make sure I finished on time.

Wendy Stoller for her skill in typesetting in the midst of my changes and conflicting schedules.

Dick Dominenta for getting me started on the book.

Tish Aaron and Phil Bishop for suggestions and support.

For former students Kadi, Pattie, Olivia, Jodi, Kristie, Janet–who typed and helped write over the years.

Aunt Helen Luntz and my grandmother Sara Wilcox for their wealth of recipes and experience.

Family, friends and students who encouraged me and wouldn't let me give up.

Kathleen Leger, Jan Lewis & the crew of Channel 36 TV – "Todays Kitchen" for their help in getting the recipes out to my TV public

"Be delighted with the Lord. Then He will give you all your heart's desires. Commit everything you do to the Lord. Trust Him to help you do it and He will." Psalms 37:4,5

I know the plans I have for you says the Lord – plans for your good to give you a hope & a future.
Jeremiah 29:11

In Fond Memory
of
two of my dearest companions

<u>Sweet Sam</u> - my beautiful buff cocker who at 5½ years gave up his battle with lymphoma on February 21, 1990

<u>Sasha</u> <u>Girlie Girl</u> - our cute black 2½ year old cocker who died 5 days later on February 26th. She must have needed to be with SAM!

Carol Lee   Bob   Sonia Pussycat

<u>Happy Footnote</u>: To help everyone's sorrow and mend broken hearts we discovered <u>Samantha</u> & <u>Sabrina</u> in Oregon - 2 six week old cocker sisters. They are dark buff color and precious puppies.

Sonia pussycat is not too over joyed with the chore of breaking in 2 new puppies again!

TABLE OF CONTENTS

INTRODUCTION

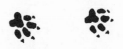

INSPIRATION AND STYLE

This cookbook really began in my childhood home. I grew up in the type of family where holiday celebrations were centered around preparing and enjoying good meals. Our tables were always laden with the best of everything. But what I remember most are my Mother's pies, Aunt Helen's cakes, and Grandmother's cookies, rolls and jelly.

Home was a great inspiration, but my real training started after college when I began cooking for a living. As an Edison Home Economist I gave cooking demonstrations and taught people how to use and care for new electric appliances like the microwave ovens which hit the markets in the early 1960's.

The book idea was born when my college foods classes started testing and generating popular food creations. As the recipe development continued our audience increased and the demand for the recipes caused me to set up a public file. One thing led to another and a few of my students and I began writing for Karlin's Kitchen.

That was about 15 years ago. But because of teaching and family responsibilities the book was always pushed to the back burner. In January of 1985 Karlin's Kitchen started to gel when I realized I'd never get it done unless I chose to make the time. It was then the Lord provided me with the right people to start the "presses" rolling. As I'm putting the final touches on it I am still amazed at the miracle. It has been a thrill to see a good team of people brought together at the right time to create a great book.

Karlin's Kitchen is unique from other cookbooks because most of the recipes have stood the test of time and experience. Not only have they been tested over and over by 1,000's of students in my college foods classes but they have been used and evaluated in homes by their families and friends.

As a result of my teaching experiences I understand the problems people have reading recipes and preparing food. The recipe style is my best effort to give you the clearest direction possible. Because I've lived through my students' problems, I've added many tips, recommendations, and special helps to head off difficulties. I also tried to share with you some of the valuable information I've learned over the years.

I hope you enjoy using this special collection. The recipes that were selected are meant to provide you with basically good food that is typical of what comes out of my own Karlin's Kitchen day after day. It is my wish to help you have many creative hours that you can share with your family and friends. "Bon Appetit!"

PERSONAL TIPS FROM THE KARLIN HOUSEHOLD

Greetings from my house to yours. My cat, Sonia Pussycat, has spent a great deal of time walking over my work as I've been writing and Sam, my Buff Cocker has kept all our spirits up by his childlike antics during the pressure of these final days of production. Here are some personal suggestions from me to you, that will help you enjoy a richer, yet safer, experience in the kitchen.

1. Please look over the contents of this book and avail yourself of the various SPECIAL HELPS that have been included for your benefit – mainly food prep terms, equivalents, some basic nutrition and diet information.
2. Karlin's Kitchen is not intended to be a "Bible" of cooking, rather a special collection to be used *with* a general all-purpose cookbook.
3. Please read the TIPS with each section to insure success with certain complex techniques – egg foams, yeast breads, pastries.
4. Realize that serving amounts given will be relative to the hands that make the food and how much gets eaten as you are cooking. In our house we have been bothered by a phantom who raids the refrigerator at odd hours particularly looking for peanut butter. I accuse my husband, but he blames Mattie, my cleaning lady of 17 years. It's interesting though, I found out she doesn't eat peanut butter – maybe Sam the dog?!
5. The cooking times might need adjusting depending on your food temperature and your equipment difference, oven size and calibration.
6. Please be safety conscious. Most home accidents occur in the kitchen. Follow proper safety rules particularly with knives, hot fat, boiling mixtures and electric equipment.
7. Careful sanitation is a must. Insist on a clean you (hands), a clean kitchen, clean food, and clean equipment to insure safe meals.

SUCCESSFUL RECIPE PROCEDURE

Planning ahead not only saves your time, money and energy but is the real key to success. A positive attitude will help you learn new techniques and enjoy what you are doing.

1. Read the entire recipe through before you do anything so you can: SHOP WISELY, check out EQUIPMENT NEEDS, and ORGANIZE YOUR PROCEDURE.
2. Estimate your TIME wisely by remembering to plan for: Your EXPERIENCE level, SEQUENCE of recipe (hours for chilling, etc.), COOKING DELAYS (slow yeast breads, etc.) and CLEAN UP TIME.
3. Get ORGANIZED by doing things IN ORDER and not at the last minute – arranging oven racks, preheating and planning for and preparing equipment ahead.
4. Don't COMPROMISE recipes by eliminating steps (sifting and measuring) or changing technique or timing because you're in a hurry.
5. READ FOOD LABELS carefully so you use the correct ingredients (unsweetened chocolate vs. semi-sweet).
6. Don't SUBSTITUTE INGREDIENTS unless you know what you're doing (all recipes require LARGE EGGS, FRESH lemon juice, FRESH parsley, LEAF herbs – not ground unless specified).
7. Don't substitute measuring equipment or change pan size because recipe will bake differently and times will be altered.
8. Clean up well as you go along since you might need to reuse equipment and unclean bowls or beaters might cause failure.

EQUIPMENT NEEDS

You cannot even hope for success if you "compromise" or fail to use the proper cooking equipment. This is especially crucial for pan size and type (ie. glass vs. metal), all measuring equipment and certain recommended utensils which insure the proper results.

If your oven isn't working properly your baked goods may fail or burn. Following is a list of recommendations for stocking your kitchen.

- Standard measuring spoons
- Glass liquid measures 1, 2, & 4 cup
- Dry measures in units for leveling
- Wire whips
- Wooden spoons
- Rubber spatulas
- Tongs
- 4–5 decent knives
- Serrated slicing knife
- Sifter
- Kitchen shears
- Meat and yeast thermometer
- Metal grater
- Various spatulas
- Rolling pin
  Pastry blender
- Glass mixing bowls
- Metal mixing bowls
  Copper beating bowl
  Soup ladle
- Pastry brush
- Chopping board
- Sauté skillets with lids 6, 8, 10, 12 inch
  Cast Iron Skillet
- Complete set of stainless steel pots & pans – inc.double boiler
  Large Soup kettle with lid
- Electric hand mixer
  Food processor
  Blender
  Heavy duty electric mixer
- Glass and metal baking pans – 13 x 9 inches
- Casseroles or soufflé shaped casseroles
- Jelly roll pan
- Cookie sheets
- Roasting rack
- Broiling pan
- Glass pie plates – 9 inch
  Mini muffin tins
  Cooling racks
- Minute timers
  Skewers

- ABSOLUTE MUSTS

SPECIAL MENU PLANNING

MENUS FOR EVERYDAY

These menus I might prepare on the spur of the moment or for friends that we invite to our house for dinner. * Indicate Recipes from Karlin's Kitchen

Country Meat Loaf*
Green Beans Supreme*
Corn on the Cob
Fruit & Ice Cream
Merlot

Herbed Broiled Fish*
Rice Pilaff*
Tomato & Cucumber Salad
Fruit & Cheese
Fumé Blanc, Muscadet

Broiled Lobster
Caesar Salad a la Karlin*
Hot Bread
Fresh Fruit
Chardonnay

Bob's Spaghetti*
Mixed Green Salad
Garlic Bread*
Chianti, Zinfandel

Veal Nicoise*
Buttered Noodles
Sauteed Vegetables*
Rosé or Red Rhone

Oven Fried Chicken*
Green Beans with Sauteed
 Onions & Mushrooms*
Biscuits with Gravy
Fresh Fruit Salad
Young Red Wine

Pork Chops with Wine and
 Herbs*
Vegetable Rice*
Mixed Green Salad
Audrey's Cobbler*
Chenin Blanc, Fumé Blanc

Roast Beef with Potatoes &
 Onions*
Italian Green Bean Salad*
Fresh Fruit & Ice Cream
Cabernet or Pinot Noir

BBQ Steak
Mother's Fresh Fried
 Potatoes*
Company Broccoli*
Young Cabernet, Burgundy

Chicken Soup with Matzo
 Balls*
Fruit & Cheese
Fumé Blanc, Rosé

Ham*
Ratatouille*
Hot Bread
Fresh Fruit Salad
Rosé

Quesadillas*
Beef Tortilla Casserole*
Pineapple Cabbage Salad*
Rosé or Burgundy

Pasta & Shrimp*
Italian Mixed Green Salad
Hot Sourdough Bread
Fumé Blanc, Rosé
Beaujolais

Pork Roast
Grits Soufflé*
Steamed Broccoli
Fresh Fruit Salad
Chardonnay

Prosciutto & Melon
Scampi*
Pasta with Cheese
Mixed Green Salad
Fumé Blanc, Soave

Roast Chicken & Potatoes
Frances Suprise Casserole*
Cranberry Salad*
Chardonnay, Beaujolais

Chicken a la Karlin*
Mixed Green Salad
Sourdough Bread
Zinfandel

Split Pea Soup*
Singapore Chicken Salad*
Hot Rolls
Gewurztraminer, Rosé

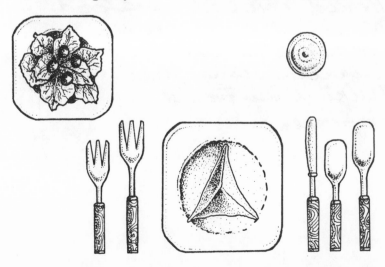

SPECIAL OCCASIONS

These menus are planned to give you an idea of what might be served at Holidays and other special celebrations. * Indicate recipes from Karlin's Kitchen

Antipasto Salad
Choppino*
Hot Sour Dough
   Bread
Fruit and Cheese
Chianti or Zinfandel

Veal Shish Kabob*
Ratatouille*
Stuffed Zucchini*
Hot Bread
Fruit and Cheese
Rosé or Red Rhone

Baked Stuffed Salmon*
Cauliflower Parmesan*
Mushroom Salad on Tomatoes*
Wiki Wiki Fruit Salad*
Chardonnay or French Chablis

Poulet au Fromage*
Mushroom Rice Pilaff*
Mixed green with
   canteloupe and
   tomatoes
Fresh Fruit Pie*
*Chardonnay or Pinot
   Noir*

Baked Ham*
Zucchini Soufflé*
Baked Beans*
Potato Salad*
Fresh Fruit Salad
Hot Rolls*
Cherry Pie*
German White, Rosé

Roast Prime Rib*
Creamed Spinach*
Yorkshire Pudding*
Salad Chez Karlin*
Fruit Cream Cheese Pie*
*Cabernet Sauvignon or
   Pinot Noir*

BBQ Steak with Herb
   butter*
Stuffed Baked
   Potatoes
Salad Chez Karlin*
Vanilla Ice Cream
   with Hot Chocolate
   Sauce*
*Young Cabernet
   Savignon*

Zucchini Soup*
Roast Turkey with
   stuffing*
Mashed Potatoes and
   Gravy*
Cranberry Sauce
Sweet Potato Soufflé*
Relishes
Pumpkin Pie*
*Chardonnay or
   Zinfandel*

BBQ Ribs*
BBQ Chicken
Grits Soufflé*
Marinated Salad*
Garlic Bread*
Peach Cobbler*
Rosé or Fume Blanc

Brunch
Sour Cream Coffee Cake
Fresh Fruit
Cheese Bake
Lox & Bagels
Mimosas

Paella*
Mixed Green Salad
Sherbet Torte*
Spanish Red or Rosé

Salad Buffet
Chinese Chicken
Baked Avocado Seafood
Marinated Vegetable
Cucumber Ring
Curried Tuna Rice
Wiki Wiki Fruit
Popovers

APPETIZERS

Appetizers are enjoyed worldwide, but have become more significant in the American diet with the advent of "grazing" – people eating smaller amounts on the run to fit into their lifestyle.

Remember when serving appetizers that their purpose is to enhance your gathering. Never overfill your guests or duplicate food if a main meal is to follow. This is a perfect opportunity to be creative. Use garnishes to make a presentation tempting to the eye and palate of your guests.

MY "FAMOUS" CHEESE

TIP: This freezes well for a month or so and keeps in the refrigerator for 2 weeks.

Looks and tastes great stuffed in celery and then cut up in small pieces.

Makes 4 small glasses.

I have made this recipe and given it as Christmas gifts for years, but never would give out the recipe. As a result, it has become very "famous" even among my friends' children, who wait for it every year.

2 cups sharp cheddar cheese, grated
1 (8 oz.) package cream cheese
1 cube butter
1 tablespoon prepared mustard
3 tablespoons brandy, or to taste
1/8 teaspoon cayenne pepper
 4-5 small jars

1. Beat cheeses and butter until fairly smooth.
2. Add remaining ingredients and beat until spreading consistency.
3. Pack into small glasses. Seal with plastic wrap and keep refrigerated. Serve at room temperature.

CURRY-OLIVE SPREAD

Good cold on crackers, stuffed in celery or spread on English muffins and broiled.

2 cups grated cheddar cheese
2 tablespoons butter
½ cup mayonnaise
1 teaspoon curry powder
1 cup chopped black olives
½ cup chopped green onions

1. In a medium bowl, beat (with an electric mixer if possible) grated cheese, butter, mayonnaise and curry powder till light and fluffy.
2. Fold in drained olives and onions. Use as desired.

BACON-OLIVE SPREAD

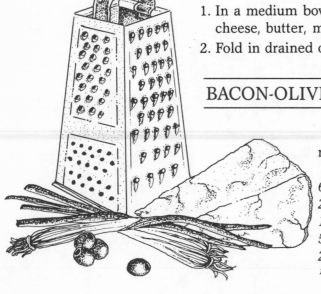

Good stuffed in celery sticks, in cherry tomatoes or rolled in balls and put on pretzel sticks.

6 ounces cream cheese, softened
2 tablespoons mayonnaise
1 teaspoon Worcestershire sauce
5 slices bacon, fried and crumbled
2 tablespoons minced green onion
¼ cup chopped black olives
 seasoned pepper (optional)

1. Beat the first three ingredients together until smooth. Blend in bacon, onion and olives. Taste for seasoning. Serve as desired.

SMOKED SALMON SPREAD

This mixture can be shaped into a log or a ball, or it may be served as a spread with crackers or on cucumber slices.

1   pound canned salmon
1   (8 oz.) package cream cheese, softened
1   tablespoon lemon juice
2   tablespoons grated onion
1   teaspoon prepared horseradish
¼   teaspoon salt
¼   teaspoon liquid smoke
3   tablespoons chopped parsley

1. Drain and flake salmon, removing any skin and bones.
2. Combine salmon with softened cream cheese, lemon juice, onion, horseradish, salt and liquid smoke. Mix thoroughly and chill, wrapped in plastic wrap.
3. Shape chilled salmon mixture into a ball or log and roll in parsley. Serve chilled.

TUNA SPREAD

Makes 3 cups   Delicious served on cucumber slices and garnished with pieces of olive or pimiento.

2   (7 oz.) cans tuna, drained
6   ounces cream cheese, softened
½   cup mayonnaise
1   small onion, sliced
½   teaspoon pepper
¼   teaspoon Tabasco sauce
½   pound fresh mushrooms, chopped
2   tablespoons butter
3   tablespoons chopped parsley
     electric mixer

1. Put tuna, cream cheese, mayonnaise, onion, pepper and Tabasco sauce into a mixing bowl. Beat with an electric mixer until smooth.
2. Saute mushrooms in butter until brown.
3. Add parsley and mushrooms to tuna mixture. Blend well.
4. Chill until serving time.

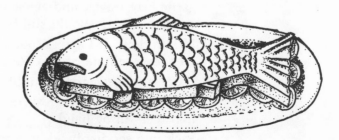

"PARTY" CHEESE BALL

TIP: This cheese is best if served at room temperature.

So much better if home made.

1   (8 oz.) package cream cheese, softened
1   cup cheddar cheese, grated*
1   tablespoon mayonnaise
1   teaspoon Worcestershire sauce
3   drops Tabasco sauce
1/8 teaspoon garlic powder
1/8 teaspoon paprika
    chopped parsley

*For variation use ¼ cup bleu cheese.

1. Blend well all ingredients, except parsley. Roll into a ball.
2. Wrap in plastic wrap and chill until the ball is well shaped. Roll in chopped parsley before serving.

PATE A LA KARLIN

I don't usually like liver but this combination is so good that very few people will not like it. Serve on rye bread or crackers. This keeps refrigerated for days and freezes well for a month.

1   cube plus 2 tablespoons of butter
1   onion, chopped
1   bunch of green onions, chopped
2   chopped garlic cloves
2   bay leaves
1   pound fresh chicken livers
1   tablespoon flour
1   teaspoon salt
½   teaspoon pepper
¼   teaspoon thyme
¼   teaspoon oregano
1/8 teaspoon tarragon
3-4 tablespoons brandy
1   tablespoon green peppercorns (drained)
    food processor
    rye bread or crackers

1. In a large skillet melt butter. On medium-high heat saute onions, garlic, bay leaves, and chicken livers until onions and livers are just cooked. (Livers should still be a *little* pink.)
2. Mix in flour and spices (not peppercorns), herbs and brandy and simmer for a minute or two. Remove bay leaves.
3. Process cooked mixture until smooth.
4. At last minute, when texture is smooth enough, add peppercorns—or fold them in by hand.
5. Pack into serving bowl or crocks, cover well and chill before serving.

"EASY" PATE

Don't tell people there's liver in it and they'll love it.

1 (8 oz.) package cream cheese
1 (8 oz.) package liver sausage or Braunschweiger
1 tablespoon chopped onion
1 teaspoon lemon juice
1 teaspoon Worcestershire sauce
1 tablespoon chopped parsley
  salt and pepper to taste
  crackers for serving

1. Combine cream cheese and liver sausage.
2. Add remaining ingredients and mix well.
3. Mold or shape and chill before serving.

My neighbor Janette Miller says that her daughter Marilyn gets applause from her curling club in Seattle when she brings this easy pâté

ORIENTAL DIP

2-3 cups

An old recipe but today these flavors and textures are very "in."

½ cup chopped green onions
¼ cup chopped parsley*
1 teaspoon chopped fresh ginger
1 tablespoon soy sauce
3 tablespoons chopped water chestnuts
¼ teaspoon ground coriander
1 cup sour cream
2 tablespoons mayonnaise

*Use 2 tablespoons cilantro and 2 tablespoons of parsley, if possible.

1. Blend together all ingredients.
2. Chill well and serve with crackers, chips, or fresh raw vegetables.

Use some fresh cilantro for sure

YOGURT DIP

Really refreshing!

Fritos taste particularly good with this, or any raw vegetable if you want to be calorie conscious.

½ cup cucumber, grated
¼ cup whole green onion, chopped
¼ cup radishes, chopped
1 cup plain yogurt
  salt and pepper to taste

1. Grate cucumber and squeeze out excess moisture.
2. Mix all the vegetables into yogurt, and add salt and pepper. Chill. Taste for seasoning before serving.

TIP: This recipe can be prepared ahead of time, but the color from the radishes will eventually run into the yogurt.

HOT CRAB FONDUE DIP

TIP: This would be delicious as a crab cheese sauce over toast and it's great cold, too.

3 cups

Of all the appetizers I've served over 25 years, this has been the most popular. It helped make our Santa Monica College Home Economics Christmas party famous on campus.

*The Velveeta &
mayonaise is the
secret to this recipe*

*With an electric
range you don't
need a double
boiler - just
heat on low.*

1 (8 oz.) package Velveeta cheese
1 (7 oz.) can crab, drained and cleaned
¾ cup mayonnaise
6 whole green onions, chopped
½ loaf French bread, chunked
  toothpicks
  warming plate

1. Cut up cheese in chunks.
2. In a double boiler top, combine cheese, drained crab, mayonnaise and onions and heat gently over water until cheese melts and mixture is smooth.
3. Serve in a chafing dish or fondue pot with small chunks of French bread on toothpicks or forks.

COLD CRAB DIP

2 cups

This is easy and not too expensive since any kind of canned crab is fine. Best if made ahead so flavors can "marry."

1 (7 oz.) can crab
1 (3 oz.) package cream cheese
½ cup mayonnaise
½ cup sour cream
1 teaspoon Worcestershire sauce
1 clove garlic, crushed
¼ teaspoon Tabasco sauce
  few drops of soy sauce
  seasoned to taste

1. Drain and pick over crab to clean.
2. Mix all ingredients together.
3. Chill well before serving.

HOT PARMESAN-ARTICHOKE DIP

A great hostess gift.

2-3 cups   My friend Kristi brought this over for a snack one day and I've since taken it to many gatherings where it has been an instant success.

1   *(16 oz.) can of artichoke hearts, drained*
¾   *cup mayonnaise*
¾   *cup Parmesan cheese*
¼   *teaspoon garlic powder*
    paprika
    electric mixer
    small oven-proof dish
    French bread cubes or crackers for dipping

1. In a medium mixing bowl or food processor beat artichoke hearts until they break up.
2. Beat in mayonnaise, cheese, and garlic powder until smooth and creamy.
3. Spoon into a baking dish and sprinkle with paprika. Bake at 400º for 15 to 20 minutes or until hot, puffy, and lightly brown.
4. Serve hot in a basket surrounded by crisp small chunks of hot bread for dipping.

TIP: Heat up a small unsliced loaf of French bread and cut in 1″ squares for dipping.

Make ahead & then bake right before you serve

BLEU CHEESE-AVOCADO DIP

Delicious! Can be served as a dip with crisp, raw vegetables, or as a salad dressing.

1   *cup sour cream*
2   *tablespoons milk*
2   *tablespoons bleu cheese*
2   *tablespoons lemon juice*
½   *teaspoon salt*
1   *small garlic clove*
1   *teaspoon Worcestershire sauce*
1   *avocado, cut up*

1. Put all ingredients in a blender or food processor, except avocado. Blend well.
2. Add avocado, blend just until smooth.

TIP: If you like bits of bleu cheese you might save some or add a little to the dressing at the end.

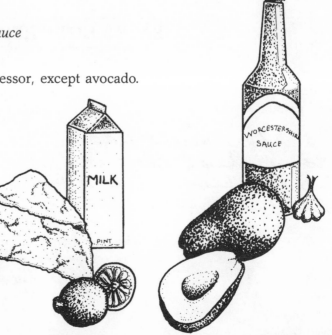

"DILLY" OF A DIP

Looks great served in a hollowed out red cabbage

Add more onion & herbs if you like

Delicious with raw vegetables, on baked potatoes or as a salad dressing.

1   cup sour cream
½   teaspoon dill weed
1   tablespoon chopped green onion
1   teaspoon Beau Monde seasoning*
½   teaspoon garlic powder
½   teaspoon seasoned salt
1   teaspoon Worcestershire sauce
     Tabasco sauce to taste

*This or Bon Appetit seasoning are brand names you should be able to find.

1. Mix together all ingredients and chill before serving.

GUACAMOLE

TIP: If you make this ahead, place plastic wrap right *on the dip* so the air won't darken it.

Good with taco chips or on a salad. Sour cream may be added to extend it.

2   ripe avocados
1   tomato, chopped
¼   cup chopped onion
1   tablespoon lemon juice
¼   teaspoon Tabasco sauce, or to taste
1   small garlic clove, crushed
     seasoned salt to taste

1. Peel and mash avocado with a fork. Add remaining ingredients and blend well.
2. Chill well before serving, if desired.

GRACE'S HOT CHEESE 'N CHILE DIP

TIP: Degree of "hotness" can be determined by the kind and amount of chiles you add.

You might add some fresh chopped up Anaheim chilies for more zip.

This is a favorite at parties with all my friends. It tastes good cold, also. Add some chopped green onions, if desired.

1   pound Velveeta cheese, cut up
1   (4 oz.) can green chiles, chopped
1   (16 oz.) can stewed tomatoes, drained and chopped
     taco chips or bread chunks for dipping
     fondue or chafing dish

1. Mix chiles and chopped tomatoes with cheese and heat carefully over water or on low heat until smooth and warm.
2. Serve fondue-style or in a chafing dish with chips or bread chunks.

SUPER NACHOS

Serves 10-12

Great for a crowd, and good left over. I got the idea for this recipe from a picture in a magazine, but I made up my own version. Everything can be prepared ahead of time, but you must assemble right before you serve. Serve as soon as possible.

TIP: Make your own home-made chips by cutting up tortillas and frying them in oil until crisp.

1 (1 lb.) can refried beans
1 pound ground meat
½ package taco seasoning*
1 onion, chopped
1½ cups grated Jack or similar cheese
1 bottle mild Mexican sauce or taco sauce
1 recipe for guacamole
½ cup sour cream
1 small can black olives
2-3 whole green onions, chopped
1 chopped tomato
   tortilla chips
1 oven proof oval serving platter or
   13 X 9" flat casserole

*Or season meat to taste.

1. Spread beans evenly over ¾ of the platter.
2. In a skillet on high heat, saute meat, taco seasoning and onion until lightly brown. Gently spoon meat mixture over layer of beans.
3. Sprinkle with cheese and taco sauce and bake at 425° until mixture is hot and cheese just melts (10-15 minutes).
4. Remove from oven and place tortilla chips around edges, standing up in layers just to touch cheese and meat.
5. Carefully put guacamole over center of dish and then make a smaller circle of sour cream on top of guacamole.
6. Decorate sour cream with olives, green onions and tomatoes, making them in the form of a cross or "X" shape neatly on the sour cream.

QUESADILLAS

6 corn or flour tortillas
1 cup Jack cheese, grated
1 (4 oz.) can diced green chiles
   chopped green onion
   butter
   Mexican salsa

1. Cover half of the tortilla with some cheese, chiles and green onion.
2. Fold tortilla in half, butter outside of tortilla and brown in skillet until cheese is melted.
3. Serve whole or cut into pieces as an appetizer. Garnish with salsa, if desired.

OLIVIA'S CERVICHE

TIP: Use frozen fish or freeze the fish for 24 hours to be sure the fish is safe to eat raw.

2 cups

Olivia is a former student who helped me with this book. This is a very popular appetizer—especially with the men. The citrus juice "cooks" the fish. Serve as a first course or with crackers. This is best if made a day ahead.

1   pound white sea bass (or any mild white fish) cut into ½ inch chunks or strips (see Tip)
3-4 lemons, juiced*
3   limes, juiced (optional)
1   large tomato, chopped
4   whole green onions, chopped
2   fresh jalapeno chiles**
     (or diced canned mild green chiles)
2   tablespoons chopped parsley
¼   cup olive oil
1   tablespoon vinegar
1   teaspoon leaf oregano
     salt and pepper to taste
1   avocado—for garnish
     *Always use fresh juice, never bottled.
     **Jalapeno chiles are dark green in color and approximately 1½ to 2 inches in length. If using fresh chiles, cut these in half and scoop out seeds, then rinse in cold water and chop.

1. Place cut up fish in a deep bowl and add enough lemon and lime juice to cover fish. Refrigerate for at least 6 hours or overnite. Stir fish in the juice every so often.
2. After marinating, remove the excess juice. Add the remainder of the ingredients except the avocado and toss gently. Taste for seasoning and refrigerate until serving time. Garnish with sliced or cubed avocado.

CAROL WALKER'S HOT OLIVE CHEESE BALLS

TIP: These can be made ahead and baked right before serving—or freeze unbaked and bake when needed.

25 balls

My husband's favorite and well worth the time to make.

1   cup grated cheddar cheese
2   tablespoons butter, softened
½   cup sifted flour
     dash of cayenne pepper
25   pimiento stuffed green olives
     baking sheet

1. Mix cheese, butter, flour and cayenne into a dough.
2. Wrap enough dough around each olive to just cover.
3. Bake in a 400° oven for 15 minutes or until brown. Serve hot.

ARTICHOKE-CHEESE BAKE

Serves 6-8   Excellent as an appetizer, warm or cold, cut up in small cubes—or as a first course or side dish.

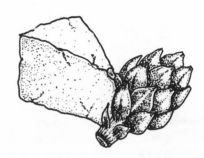

2   *(6 oz.) jars marinated artichoke hearts*
1   *medium onion, chopped*
1   *garlic clove, minced*
8   *ounces sharp cheddar cheese, grated*
4   *eggs*
¼   *teaspoon salt*
¼   *teaspoon pepper*
¼   *teaspoon leaf oregano*
¼   *teaspoon hot pepper sauce*
2   *tablespoons chopped parsley*
¼   *cup bread crumbs*
    11 X 7" baking pan

1. Preheat oven to 325⁰.
2. Drain the marinade of one jar of artichoke hearts into a skillet. Drain the other jar and reserve the artichoke hearts from both jars and set aside.
3. Saute the onion and garlic in the skillet with the marinade.
4. In a large bowl, blend the remaining ingredients together and add the sauteed onion, garlic and drained artichokes. Fold mixture together and pour into a baking pan.
5. Bake in a preheated 325⁰ oven 25 minutes, until lightly browned and mixture is set up.

GARLIC CHEESE STICKS

Serve whole, or cut in small pieces. These freeze well, unbaked.

TIP: If frozen, bake sticks on the same foil they were wrapped in.

1   *large loaf sliced sandwich bread*
1½   *cubes butter*
3   *cloves garlic, cut up*
1-2 *cups Parmesan cheese*
     baking sheet with lip, or jelly roll pan

1. Cut crusts off bread slices. With a rolling pin flatten each slice until very thin.
2. Melt the butter and add the garlic. Brush both sides of each flattened bread slice with the butter-garlic mixture.
3. Sprinkle each bread slice with Parmesan cheese and roll up from one corner to the other. Use toothpicks if necessary to hold together.
4. Place rolled up slices on a cookie sheet. Brush with more butter and sprinkle the top with cheese.
5. Bake in 375⁰ oven for 15 minutes, or until golden and somewhat crisp.

KADI'S BACON AND CHEESE ROLL-UPS

TIP: You can refrigerate these or freeze them *well wrapped* and then bake right before serving.

75-100 Roll-ups

These freeze well, or will hold refrigerated up to three days. For a variation use cream cheese and chopped olives.

1   large loaf of soft bread
1½ pounds lean bacon
1   (8 oz.) jar cheese whiz with jalapeno peppers*
    toothpicks
    rolling pin
    broiler pan with rack

    *If you can't find cheese whiz use any soft cheese with chili pepper.

1. Preheat oven to 375⁰.
2. Cut the crusts off the bread and flatten each slice with a rolling pin. Cut slices into 4 squares.
3. Cut bacon slices into thirds.
4. Spread each bread square with a little cheese. Roll-up and wrap with a bacon slice. Secure with a toothpick.
5. Place on a broiler pan and bake in a 375⁰ oven for 12-15 minutes or until bacon is crisp. Drain and serve hot.

CHEESE AND ONION SWIRLS

TIP: If you wish to do ahead, freeze unbaked rolls in the pans and bake when desired.

Makes 24 swirls

So easy to prepare and one of my most requested appetizers.

1   cup grated cheddar cheese
3   tablespoons mayonnaise
2   tablespoons minced green onion
    dash of cayenne pepper
1   large can "crescent" refrigerated dinner rolls (8 rolls)
    paprika
2   mini-muffin pans

1. Preheat oven to 375⁰.
2. Combine cheese, mayonnaise, onion, and cayenne pepper.
3. Unroll crescent rolls and divide into 4 rectangles, pressing together diagonal seam.
4. Spread cheese mixture evenly over rectangles. Roll up jelly roll style starting with the long edge. Cut roll into 6 pieces.
5. Place pieces (cut side up) in mini-muffin pans. Sprinkle with paprika and bake at 375⁰ for 10-12 minutes or until golden brown.
6. Serve hot right out of the oven.

MINI QUICHES

These can be baked ahead and reheated if necessary

Makes 36

Pastry can be made ahead and rolled out when ready to bake. Try to serve them hot from the oven.

TIP: You'll have to do this in batches unless you have lots of pans. The bacon could be cooked on paper plates and paper towels in the microwave if you have one.

double crust pie pastry (see pastry)
4   strips bacon*
1   cup light cream or milk
2   eggs at room temperature
¼   teaspoon salt
¼   teaspoon dry mustard
    few dashes cayenne pepper
2   cups Swiss cheese grated
    2½″ biscuit cutter
    mini-muffin pans
    rolling pin and cloth

Substitute some finely chopped green onion or turkey ham if you prefer to the bacon

Bacon may be omitted if you prefer.

1. Fry bacon until crisp, drain on paper towels and crumble.
2. Roll out pastry to thickness thinner than for a pie—about 1/8 of an inch.
3. Cut 2½″ circles with biscuit cutter. Line mini-muffin pans with pastry circles and chill pastry for 10 to 15 minutes before filling.
4. Preheat oven to 400⁰ while pastry is chilling.
5. Beat together cream, eggs, salt, mustard, and cayenne pepper.
6. Place a little grated cheese and bacon in each pastry round. Pour beaten cream mixture in each to half full.
7. Bake at 400⁰ for 15 minutes, or until golden brown and filling is just set.

TOMATO BOMBS

Liz the book lady at Hinsley's in Santa Monica loves this recipe, & sells lots of books because of it! Thanks Liz for being such a great friend.

The bomb comes from the Tabasco sauce.

cherry tomatoes
bacon (one strip per each 6 tomatoes)
Tabasco sauce
cheddar or Jack cheese, grated
(1 cup per each 30 tomatoes)

1. Cut off tops and carefully clean out centers of tomatoes with a spoon or melon baller.
2. Cook bacon until crisp, drain on paper towels and crumble.
3. Place one drop of Tabasco sauce in each tomato.
4. Sprinkle some crumbled bacon in each tomato, and fill with grated cheese.
5. Broil *until cheese just begins to melt*—a few minutes. Serve hot.

MUSHROOM TURNOVERS

TIP: Always sift flour before measuring in *all* recipes for accuracy.

Makes 35-40

These take time and a little skill—but they are really fabulous. You can freeze them unbaked but they should be baked right before serving.

1   cup butter (2 cubes) slightly softened
1   (8 oz.) package softened cream cheese
½   teaspoon salt
2   cups sifted flour (see Tip)
    pastry cloth and sleeve
    rolling pin
    2½" inch biscuit cutter

1. In a mixing bowl beat the butter, cheese and salt until smooth. Blend in the flour until pastry has a smooth texture.
2. Partially flatten the pastry between plastic wrap and chill until it will roll easily and can be handled. (This can be overnite or put the wrapped dough in the freezer while you make the filling.)
3. When the dough is ready to handle, roll out *one half* of it on a floured pastry cloth to about a 9" by 6" rectangle. Fold in thirds, re-roll, fold again and roll dough to 1/8" thickness.
4. Using a round cookie or biscuit cutter, cut 2½ inch rounds. Re-roll the trimmings and the rest of the dough when ready and continue to cut into rounds.

Mushroom Filling

Make while pastry is chilling or make ahead and keep chilled.

2   (4 oz.) cans mushrooms, drained and minced
½   cup minced onion
2   tablespoons butter
½   teaspoon salt
1/8 teaspoon white pepper
1   teaspoon lemon juice
2   teaspoons flour
½   cup light cream
1   tablespoon sherry

1. In a small saucepan, saute the minced mushrooms and onions in the butter for 5 minutes.
2. Stir in salt, pepper, lemon juice and flour. Simmer for 2 minutes.
3. Slowly blend in cream. Simmer and stir until thickened. Stir in sherry, remove from heat and chill filling.

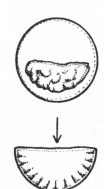

Assembling Turnovers
    350° oven
    fork
    cookie sheets
    egg wash—egg yolk and 1 tablespoon milk
    pastry brush

1. Put about a *level* teaspoon of filling off center of each pastry round. *Don't fill too full.* Moisten inner edges of rounds with water and fold one side over to the other. Press edges together with fork to seal.
2. Carefully place turnovers on a lightly greased baking sheet. Brush with egg and chill 1 hour or overnite. (Freeze them at this point on the sheets, wrapped well.)
3. Bake in a preheated 350⁰ oven 25 to 30 minutes or until golden. *Serve hot.*

Watch all your work disappear in minutes!

CHEESE FILOS

75-100 filos

Worth the time! This is one of the best recipes for this Greek-style appetizer. They can be made ahead, frozen and then baked or reheated.

TIP: These take time to prepare and are best made with the help of a friend.

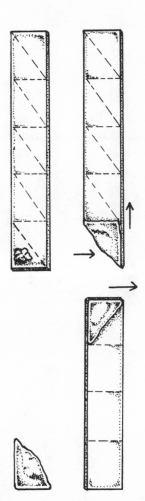

6   *medium russet potatoes, peeled and cooked*
½   *pound feta cheese, chopped*
5   *eggs, beaten*
⅓   *cup freshly grated Romano or Parmesan cheese*
¼   *cup butter (½ cube) softened*
3   *tablespoons finely chopped parsley*
    salt to taste (1-2 teaspoons)
1   *pound fresh filo dough*
    oil and melted butter (1-2 cups)
    grated Romano or Parmesan cheese
    pastry brush
    electric beater or food processor
    jelly roll pans

1. In a large bowl, mash hot potatoes and beat in feta cheese.
2. Beat in eggs, ⅓ cup cheese, butter and parsley until mixture is fairly smooth. Add salt to taste.
3. Lay out filo dough one sheet at a time, keeping remaining dough covered with damp towel to prevent drying.
4. Cut each sheet into 2-inch strips. Brush each strip with oil-butter mixture and sprinkle with a little cheese.
5. Place 1 teaspoon of filling in corner of the 2" dough strip. Fold from top to bottom, corner to corner, as you would fold a flag. Fold as tightly as possible. Place triangle on a jelly roll pan.
6. Preheat oven to 375⁰.
7. Continue folding dough as fast as possible. When baking pan is full, sprinkle triangles with cheese. Bake at 375⁰ for 25-30 minutes or until lightly browned and the filling is set.

STUFFED MUSHROOMS "A LA KARLIN"

TIP: Make them ahead and broil right before serving.

For a nice change stuff mushrooms w/ crab imperial on p. 96

I prefer thyme or mixed herbs - since tarragon is too predominate for my taste!

Serves 6-8

A result of combining a few persons' ideas. Good as hors d'oeuvres or as a vegetable side dish.

20 large mushrooms
2 tablespoons soft bread crumbs
¼ cup grated Parmesan cheese
¼ cup grated Swiss cheese
½ cube softened butter
3 tablespoons chopped green onion
2 tablespoons chopped parsley
2 tablespoons Sherry wine
¼ teaspoon garlic powder
1/8 teaspoon ~~tarragon~~ *thyme or herb of choice*
   seasoned salt and pepper
   flat pan for broiling

1. Wash and dry the mushrooms. Remove stems and finely chop them.
2. In a mixing bowl, gently combine the chopped stems, bread crumbs, cheese, butter, onion, parsley, wine, garlic and tarragon. Season to taste.
3. Fill each mushroom cap with some of the mixture and arrange them on the broiling pan.
4. Broil about 3 inches from heat, 5-7 minutes or till hot and slightly brown. Serve hot.

PARTY MEATBALLS

If you are serving a crowd you better make plenty - because they go fast

TIP: These freeze well after browning. Just wrap well and reheat in microwave or in a sauce.

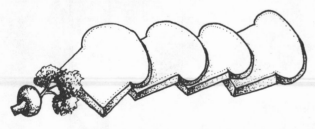

30-40

Good served plain or in a BBQ or marinara sauce.

4 slices of bread
2 eggs, beaten
½ cup water
1 pound ground beef
¼ cup Parmesan cheese
2 tablespoons chopped parsley
½ teaspoon salt
¼ teaspoon pepper
¼ teaspoon Italian herbs
½ teaspoon Worcestershire sauce
   non-stick skillet

1. Soak bread slices in ½ cup water 2 to 3 minutes. Add the eggs and mix well.
2. Mix in ground beef, cheese, and remaining seasonings to taste.
3. With wet hands, form meat mixture into small balls about 1" round.
4. Brown meatballs well in a non-stick skillet. Serve hot on toothpicks.

BEVERAGES & WINES

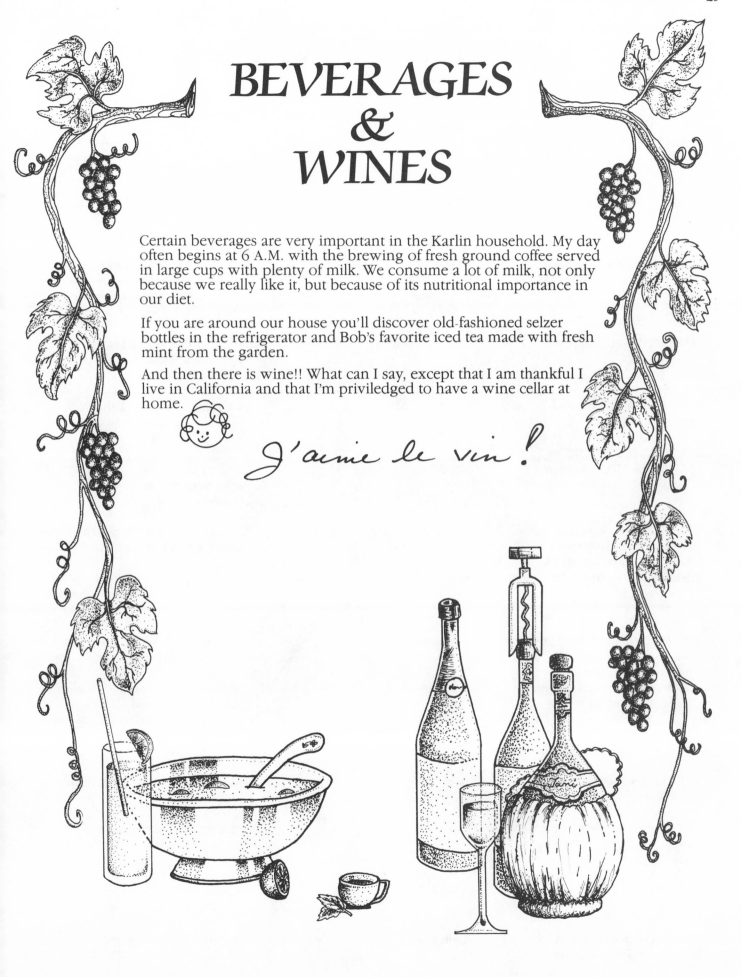

Certain beverages are very important in the Karlin household. My day often begins at 6 A.M. with the brewing of fresh ground coffee served in large cups with plenty of milk. We consume a lot of milk, not only because we really like it, but because of its nutritional importance in our diet.

If you are around our house you'll discover old-fashioned selzer bottles in the refrigerator and Bob's favorite iced tea made with fresh mint from the garden.

And then there is wine!! What can I say, except that I am thankful I live in California and that I'm priviledged to have a wine cellar at home.

J'aime le vin!

EASY TO USE WINE GUIDE

GRAPE VARIETY	DESIGNATION/GENERIC	MENU OR SUGGESTED FOODS
CHARDONNAY★—Dry, but rich. Complex vanilla, apple, pear aromas.	White Burgundy Chablis	Elegant poultry, herb-stuffed chicken, fish with substance, grilled swordfish, oysters, pastas with lobster, cold salmon.
CHENIN BLANC—Dry or sweet fruity wine.	Middle Loire (Vouvray)	Appetizers, fish, Chinese food, curry, light dishes, dessert souffles.
GEWURZTRAMINER★— Spicy, fruity, but dry. Rich, but soft.	Alsace	Charcroute garnie, sausages, curry, Mexican food, Chinese food, pork roast, ham, picnics, seafood, smoked fish.
MUSCADET—Light, dry, crisp wines.	West Loire (Brittany)	Seafood from same region, oysters, mussels, clams, simple seafood, ham.
RIESLING★—Sweet-acid balance. Fruity.	Germany, Alsace	German-style food, fish, chicken, light meats, carrots, quiches, apertif.
SAUVIGNON BLANC or FUME BLANC—Aromatic, flinty, herbaceous, grassy-scented	Loire, Bordeaux	Grilled seafoods, poultry with light herb sauces, goat cheese, quiches.
SEMILLON ★ ★—Luscious, sweet wines. Sauternes, Savignon Blanc blends.	Bordeaux	Apertif or dessert wine when sweet, roquefort cheese.
GRENACHE—Strong, fruity, but pale. Rose, blended wines.	Southern France	Goes with anything, best with picnic foods, hamburgers, brunch dishes.
CABERNET SAUVIGNON★ ★ • —Great character, spicy, herbaceous, tannic.	Bordeaux	Elegant beef dishes, lamb, game, soft ripened cheese, bleu cheese.
GAMAY—The Beaujolais grape. Light, fragrant wines.	Beaujolais	Serve chilled, if desired, with tomato, spiced seafood dishes, poultry, veal, goat's milk cheese, dishes demanding a young red wine.
MERLOT★ •—Great fragrance, soft wines.	Bordeaux	Meat dishes, duck, veal, meat loaf, steaks.
PINOT NOIR★ ★ •—Complex wines, used for champagne & famous distinct reds.	Burgundy	Elegant veal, venison, quail, steak, roasts, escargot, coq au vin, cheese souffle.
SIRAH★—Heavy purple robust wines (i.e. Chateauneuf-du-Pape)	Rhone	Beef steaks, strong acidic cheeses (English cheese).
ZINFANDEL★•—Heavy, dark, fruity, berry wines, brambleberry.	California	Italian dishes, spicy meat dishes, cheese with fruit, roast chicken or turkey.

(Left margin: WHITE WINE for rows Chardonnay through Semillon; RED WINE for rows Grenache through Zinfandel)

★ TAKES SOME TIME   ★ ★ AGES WELL   • USED FOR BLUSH WINE

HOW TO MAKE A GOOD CUP OF COFFEE

A good cup of coffee should have a fragrant, heady aroma that pleases the palate even before the cup is raised to the lips. It should have a full-bodied coffee-flavor regardless of the blend with no hint of bitterness or off taste. The brew should be clear and sparkling with no evidence of floating grounds or cloudiness.

WHEN BREWING COFFEE

1. Begin with a good quality coffee that is as fresh as possible. The enemies of coffee are time and air.
2. Match the grind to the coffee pot, because the coffee must be fine enough for the water to circulate freely in order to extract all the flavor.
3. The absolute cleanliness of the coffeemaker is essential.
4. Experiment to get the strength desired.
5. If possible, try not to use less than three-quarters of any coffeemaker's capacity with the exception of Melita-type filter pots.
6. Use freshly drawn, cold water—preferably good drinking water to insure the best taste.
7. Serve coffee as soon after brewing as possible.
8. Once brewed, coffee should never be allowed to boil.

Grind your own beans right before you make coffee to get the best flavor & aromatic experience.

BEV'S SANGRIA

2 quarts   A refreshing change and nice in a punch bowl for a party.

Dry white or blush wine may be substituted if you prefer.

1 cup fresh orange juice
½ cup fresh lemon juice
¼ cup sugar
1 bottle of dry, full bodied red wine
1 quart bottle soda water
orange or lemon slices for garnish
large bowl for mixing

1. Mix juices and sugar in the punch bowl. Blend in wine and mix well.
2. Right before serving, blend in soda water to taste. Float lemon or orange slices in bowl or in individual servings.

MRS. KELLOGG'S FRUIT PUNCH

TIP: These juices can be varied, but these four are a particularly good combo.

On my way home from grade school, I used to stop at Carol's house and her mom always had this punch plus other goodies to eat. This beverage is popular with every age.

1   cup grape juice
1   (3 oz.) can frozen lemonade concentrate, mixed with 3 cans of water
1   (3 oz.) can frozen orange juice concentrate, mixed with 2 cans of water
⅓   cup bottled Hawaiian punch concentrate*
2   cups water (only if Hawaiian concentrate is used)
1   bottle club soda (optional—if fizz is desired) lemon slices for garnish

*If concentrate isn't available, make up frozen Hawaiian punch and use 2-3 cups with other juices.

1. Mix all ingredients together, except soda water. Taste and add soda if desired.
2. Chill, add ice cubes and serve.

WASSAIL PUNCH

20-30 servings

This hot punch must be brewed in a percolator. The recipe is for a 30-cup pot. This is good cold if any is left over.

3   cups grapefruit juice
7   cups orange juice
6   cups apple cider
¾   cup cold water
¾   cup sugar
12   whole cloves
2   cinnamon sticks
   30-cup coffee percolator

1. Combine fruit juices and water in a clean coffee percolator.
2. Place sugar and spices in the strainer of the percolator and perk until cycle is completed.
3. Clean strainer. Put spices in the pot and serve punch hot from the coffee pot.

SOUPS

I really like the Fall and Winter months because our California weather cools off a bit. It gives those of us who love Autumn leaves, crisp weather, and log fires a chance to get creative in the kitchen with a big kettle of soup.

When a recipe calls for stock, or broth it's basically the same thing.

Homemade is always best because you can control the salt and flavorings — but since most of us don't have the time its OK to substitute ready made.

Be very selective because some brands are far superior to others.

This a very popular dinner meal at our house

BOB'S CHICKEN SOUP

10 quarts

This soup has a bit of stormy history at our house. I never wanted to make it because it takes so much time and is such a mess to clean up. My husband likes it so much that he now shops, cooks and cleans up. I make the matzo balls and organize the presentation and the storage of the leftovers—*and of course I give advice through the whole procedure.*

Chicken soup is supposed to cure all your ills, and maybe it does! You can vary the ingredients but his formula after years of experimenting is the best, I think.

TIP: You must time your preparation and service of this dish carefully, since the stock takes at least 3 hours. The matzo balls need to be started 1½ hours ahead of serving time. Don't forget to cook the noodles and vegetables at the end, too!

Bob has discovered that wrapping the chicken in cheese cloth like the vegetables works even better. Just duplicate the procedure on the chicken like the vegetables in step #3.

16   quart soup kettle with lid
1   (5-6 pounds) roasting chicken
2-4 pieces of chicken
1   small soup bone——→ *(optional)*
    cheesecloth and string
1   tablespoon dill weed
1   tablespoon peppercorns
4   large carrots, cut up*
2   large onions, quartered
½   bunch parsley
4   stalks celery, cut up*
3   bay leaves
1   small parsnip or turnip
1   tablespoon salt
1   cup white wine
    water to cover
    matzo balls (use double recipe on matzo meal box)
    noodles
    plastic storage containers

*Plan to add a few extra vegetables at the end, if desired.

1. Wash chicken and place in the kettle with the soup bone.
2. Cut a small piece (4" X 4") of cheesecloth and make a pouch around the dill weed and peppercorns. Tie with a string.
3. Spread out a large piece of double cheesecloth (16" X 16"). Lay all the cut up vegetables, bay leaves, and herb pouch on the cheesecloth. Draw up cloth around veggies to make a large sack. Tie string around ends firmly so you can lift bag by the handle you have made.
4. Place vegetable bag in soup pot. Add salt, wine and water to cover (about 5 to 6 quarts, so pan is very full).
5. Cover and bring soup to a boil. Turn down to maintain a very gentle simmer. *Soup stock should never boil—just gently bubble.*
6. Skim off foam or top film as it forms and continue to simmer on low for *at least 3 hours.*
7. After 1 or 2 hours, start to skim off fat that accumulates and save some if you are making matzo balls.

8. About ½ hour before serving, gently remove *chicken bag &* ~~vegetable bag~~ from broth. Set in a bowl and save any vegetables you want to eat—most will be too soft.

9. Carefully remove chicken. As soon as possible, take the meat off the bones into a serving dish. Strain broth with slotted spoon or a sieve.

10. Put broth back on burner and add any raw vegetables that people want for their soup—carrots, celery, etc.

11. Put cooked matzo balls in broth and when ready, serve hot soup over noodles and chicken in large bowls and as my husband says, *"you should enjoy."*

Storing Suggestions

1. Right before you sit down to eat, fill your sink with ice cold water and put the ¾-full kettle with remaining stock carefully into the sink.

2. Replace the sink water if it gets too warm.

3. After dinner, the stock should be cool enough to ladle into Tupperware or desired sized containers for storage.

4. Portion out left-over matzo balls into soup and seal, label and store in containers. *Portion out left over chicken & noodles*

5. Soup will refrigerate for a week or freeze for months. *into soup as well since they freeze fine.*

Save all the skin & spare chicken for a gourmet treat for your pets. Make sure all the bones are removed since they are not safe for dogs to eat.

If you prepare this for Passover you cannot use noodles. Just serve the clear broth with Matzo Balls.

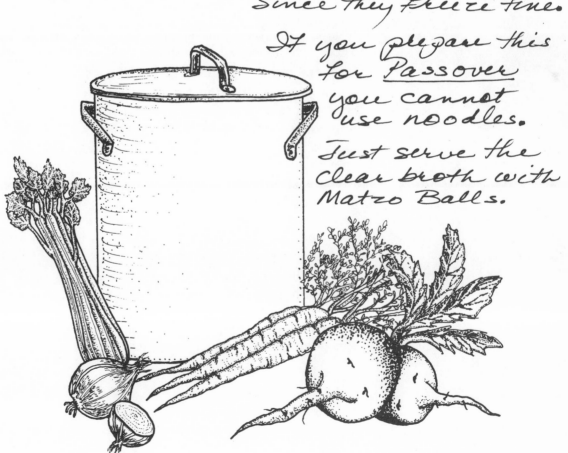

NEW ENGLAND CLAM CHOWDER

TIP: Use all milk if you prefer it not so rich.

Serves 3-4

Some corn & green onions are nice in this

This is real "white" chowder and is a recipe that people enjoy even if chowder is not their favorite. If you desire a greater quantity, this doubles easily.

¼ pound salt pork or 2 pieces bacon
1 onion, chopped
2 celery stalks, sliced
3 (6½ oz.) cans chopped or minced clams (save juice)
1 large potato, peeled and diced
¼ teaspoon seasoned salt
1/8 teaspoon white pepper
1/8 teaspoon thyme —→ *I use more thyme and sometimes "Herbs de Provence"*
1 small bay leaf
1 tablespoon butter
1 tablespoon flour*
1 cup milk
1 cup light cream
   butter for dotting
   paprika
   minced parsley

1. In a deep, large pan, cook pork until lightly brown. Remove and set aside. Save about two tablespoons of the pork fat in the pan.

2. In the fat, saute the onions and celery for a few minutes.

3. Drain the juice from the canned clams into the pan with the onions. Set clams aside.

4. Add potato, salt, pepper, thyme, bay leaf and simmer for 10 to 15 minutes or until potatoes are tender (add a little water if there is not enough liquid.)

5. If you wish to thicken the soup, mix the flour and butter together into a paste and stir into the simmering mixture. Cook for a minute or two.*

6. Now add the milk, cream and clams and heat to serving temperature over medium heat, but *do not boil.*

7. Serve in bowls or mugs, dot with butter and sprinkle with paprika and a little parsley. Add some crumbled pork if it hasn't been eaten.

*Authentic chowder is not thickened but if you desire to do so, you should at this point so the flour can cook thoroughly.

SPECIAL LENTIL SOUP

Yields 4 quarts

Delicious combination of flavors. You can cut down the amount of ham, if desired.

TIP: This is even better if made ahead of time as the flavors mellow.
Hearty red or rose.

¼   cup oil
2   cups diced cooked ham
½   pound Polish sausage, sliced
2   large onions, chopped
1   clove garlic, crushed
2   cups chopped celery
1   large tomato, chopped
1   pound lentils, washed
2   quarts water
1   cup wine
½   teaspoon tabasco sauce
1   teaspoon salt
¼   cup chopped parsley
1   (10 oz.) package frozen chopped spinach, thawed
     large sauce pot with lid

1. In a large "kettle" heat oil. Add ham, sausage, onion and garlic. Saute for 5 minutes.
2. Add celery, tomato, lentils, water, wine, tabasco, salt and parsley. Cover and simmer over low heat for 2 hours or until lentils are tender. Thin the soup with more water if necessary.
3. Add spinach and cook for 10 minutes longer.

ZUCCHINI SOUP

My friend Tru who so beautifully designed this book has a tip to give

Serves 3-4

People who don't like zucchini like this soup! It can also be made with asparagus*.

TIP: If you double this, adjust the liquid to personal taste.

1   pound zucchini, sliced
1   small onion, quartered
1   cup chicken broth
½   teaspoon salt
1/8 teaspoon pepper
½   teaspoon basil
1 ½ cups milk
½   cup cream
       blender or food processor

*For asparagus—use 1 pound of asparagus. Remove tough end of stalk and proceed as above.

Tru said "to make sure you don't fill the blender too full & please put on the lid before you turn it on unless you like soup all over you & your cookbook.

1. In a saucepan, combine zucchini, onion, chicken broth, salt, pepper and basil. Bring to a boil and simmer for 10 minutes.
2. Blend mixture in a blender or processor until smooth. With blender still running, blend in ½ cup milk.
3. Return puree to saucepan. Stir in remaining milk and cream. Heat, stirring occasionally until very hot but do not boil

MULLIGATAWNY SOUP

TIP: This soup is also great
the next day as the flavors
seem to mellow.
White Zinfandel or rose.

Serves 6-8

Delicious first course or main dish soup that is a
real hit even with people who "question" the
ingredients.

4   *tablespoons margarine or oil*
¼   *cup chopped onion*
¼   *cup diced carrots*
¼   *cup diced celery*
1   *green pepper, finely chopped*
1   *cooking apple, sliced*
1   *cup diced raw chicken*
⅓   *cup flour*
1   *teaspoon curry powder*
1/8 *teaspoon nutmeg or mace*
2   *cloves*
2   *parsley sprigs*
    salt and pepper to taste
1   *cup chopped tomatoes*
5   *cups chicken stock*
    processor or blender
    cooked rice for garnish

1. In a large saucepan, slowly saute the onion, carrots, celery, pepper, apple and chicken in the margarine for about 7 to 10 minutes.
2. Stir in the flour and then add the seasonings, tomatoes and the stock. Simmer the entire mixture for one hour.
3. Puree the cooked mixture in batches and season to taste.
4. Serve hot or cold with rice, if desired.

CABBAGE AND SAUSAGE SOUP

TIP: Add a can of white
beans to this soup to vary it.
Zinfandel, Italian red or rose.

Serves 2-3

Fun for a quick and delicious supper on a cool
evening, or when it sounds good. I make this for two
people, but just increase it for more. Crunchy bread
and fruit would be nice with this dish.

4   *Italian sausages*
1   *onion, sliced*
2   *garlic cloves, minced*
1   *cup wine (rose or red)*
1   *(16 oz.) can stewed tomatoes*
1   *cup water or chicken stock*
½   *head cabbage, sliced and shredded*
    chopped parsley

1. Cut up sausages into 2" pieces. Saute in a deep pan until they are somewhat brown. Add onion and garlic and continue to saute for about 5 minutes.
2. Add wine and simmer the mixture for about 15 minutes.

3. Add undrained tomatoes, water or stock and cabbage. Simmer for 15 to 20 minutes, until the cabbage is just tender. Add more liquid, if desired.

4. Serve hot in bowls, garnished with chopped parsley.

HEARTY SUPPER SOUP

Serves 4-6

Easy to make! Add a small salad and bread for a perfect meal.

Rose, Spanish red, young red or Zinfandel.

2	tablespoons olive oil
2	tablespoons butter
1	onion, chopped
1	pound lean ground beef
1	medium eggplant, diced
2	garlic cloves, minced
½	cup chopped carrots
½	cup sliced celery
1	(1 lb. 12 oz.) can pear shaped tomatoes (cut up)
2	(14 oz.) cans beef broth
1	teaspoon seasoned salt
1	teaspoon sugar
½	teaspoon pepper
¼	teaspoon thyme
¼	cup salad macaroni
¼	cup minced parsley
	grated Parmesan cheese
	large sauce pot with lid

1. Heat the oil and butter in a large pan. Add onion and saute for a few minutes.

2. Add the meat and stir over the heat until it loses its pinkness.

3. Add the eggplant, garlic, carrots, celery, tomatoes, beef broth, salt, sugar, pepper and thyme. Cover and simmer for about 30 minutes.

4. Add the macaroni and parsley and simmer for 10 minutes longer, or until the macaroni is tender. Serve topped with Parmesan cheese.

BROCCOLI BISQUE

TIP: Always use whole green onion in recipes unless otherwise stated.

Serves 4

Easy and delicious as a first course. Can be served warm or cold. Sour dough bread would be perfect with it.

1   (10 oz.) package frozen chopped broccoli
1   (13 oz.) can chicken broth
4   green onions, chopped
2   tablespoons chopped parsley
1   tablespoon butter
½   teaspoon salt
1   teaspoon curry powder
    pepper to taste
1   tablespoon lemon juice
    sour cream (garnish)
    chives* (garnish)
    blender or food processor

Finely chopped green onion may be substituted for chives.

1. Place broccoli in a large saucepan. Add broth, onions and parsley and bring to a boil.
2. Add butter, salt, curry powder and pepper. Simmer for 8 minutes.
3. Pour mixture into a blender or processor and blend until smooth. Add lemon juice and serve, or chill.
4. Serve soup with a dab of sour cream and sprinkle with chives, as garnish.

CUCUMBER SOUP

Serves 6-8

A wonderful first course for a special dinner. Can be served cold or hot, even though it is usually served cold.

3   cucumbers, peeled and sliced
1   leek, sliced (white part only)*
2   tablespoons butter
1   tablespoon flour
3   cups chicken stock
1   cup heavy cream
1   teaspoon dried dill weed (or two teaspoons fresh dill, chopped)
    salt and pepper to taste
1   tablespoon lemon juice
    sour cream to garnish
    chopped parsley or chopped chives
    food processor or blender

If a leek is not available, substitute 4-5 green onions, instead.

1. In a large saucepan, gently saute the cucumbers and the leek in the butter until tender—about 10 minutes. Stir in the flour and then gradually add the stock. Blend well, cover and simmer for 15 minutes.
2. Process mixture in a blender or processor until smooth. Chill until cool.
3. Stir in the cream, dill weed and season to taste with salt and pepper. Add lemon juice, if desired.
4. Chill well before serving and then garnish with sour cream and herbs.

CREAM OF MUSHROOM—CRAB BISQUE

Serves 3-4   Delicious but so simple to prepare!

¼   *pound mushrooms, sliced*
2   *tablespoons chopped onions*
2   *tablespoons butter*
2   *tablespoons flour*
2   *cups chicken broth*
¼   *teaspoon salt*
    dash ground nutmeg
1/8 *teaspoon white pepper*
3 ¼ *cups milk*
1   *cup half and half*
1   *(10½ oz.) can Cream of Asparagus soup*
1   *(7 oz.) can crab meat, drained*
1   *tablespoon chopped parsley*

1. In a large saucepan, saute mushrooms and onions in butter for a few minutes.
2. Blend in flour. Add chicken broth. Cook and stir constantly until thick and boiling.
3. Add salt, ground nutmeg, white pepper, milk, half and half, Cream of Asparagus soup and crab meat. Blend thoroughly and heat just below boiling. *Do not boil.*
4. To serve, garnish with chopped parsley.

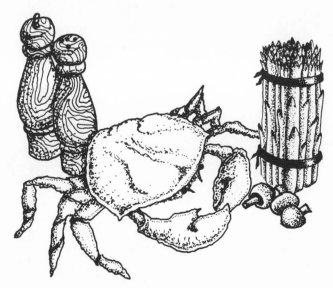

SPLIT PEA SOUP

TIP: If in a hurry step 3 & 4 can be skipped. Just add the chopped veggies to the simmering mixture.

Serves 6-8

I hate regular "peas" but I love a good dried pea soup and this combination is one that my family loves. It will keep for about a week in the refrigerator. (The latest is that my sister Trudi's cocker spaniel will not eat her kibble without this soup on it.)

white or rose

A leek gives this soup special flavor. Be sure to clean it carefully by cutting it open Lengthwise and washing out the sand that will hide in the layers.

large soup kettle
1   (1 lb.) package of dried split peas
5   cups water or chicken stock
1   cup dry Vermouth or rose wine
2   parsley sprigs, chopped
2   chopped celery stalks
1   bay leaf
½   teaspoon dried thyme
¼   teaspoon marjoram (or ½ teaspoon mixed herbs)
1   ham hock
1   strip of bacon
½   cup finely chopped carrots
½   cup chopped onions, white and green
1   large leek, chopped (white part, plus two inches of green, or 1 extra onion if leek is not available)
    salt and pepper
    chopped parsley, for garnish

I Add 1-2 teasp. more herbs.

1. Wash the split peas thoroughly under cold running water. In the soup kettle bring the water, stock and wine to a boil. Drop in the peas, parsley, celery, bay leaf, thyme, marjoram and ham hock.

2. Reduce the heat and simmer with lid "ajar" for 45 minutes to 1 hour or until the peas are just tender.

3. While the peas are simmering, cook the bacon strip in a skillet until the fat is rendered. Remove bacon and and set aside or *eat*.

4. In the bacon fat, saute the chopped carrots, onion and leek for about 5 minutes. Add these to the simmering peas.

5. Continue to simmer uncovered for another 30 minutes. If soup seems too thick add more water or wine.

6. Season to taste. Cut off meat from ham. Remove bay leaf and serve when ready.

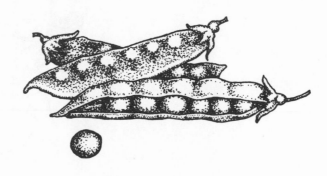

SOUPE A L'OIGNON GRATINEE

4-6 Servings   Or French Onion Soup with melted cheese. This takes a little time but the results are most satisfying.

2   tablespoons butter
2   tablespoons olive oil
1   clove garlic, minced
2   large onions, thinly sliced
½   teaspoon salt
¼   teaspoon white pepper
1   tablespoon flour
6   cups stock
½   cup wine
2   cups homemade croutons*
1-2 cups grated Swiss cheese
     oven proof soup bowls

See Caesar Salad recipe for croutons. Use olive oil instead of butter, if desired.

1. In a large saucepan, heat the butter and oil.
2. Add garlic, sliced onions, salt and pepper and slowly saute over medium heat for 20 minutes.
3. Sprinkle mixture with flour and pour in stock and wine. Bring to a boil and *simmer* covered for 15 to 20 minutes. Taste for seasoning. Stir occasionally.

Presentation
1. Place a portion of soup in oven proof tureens or soup bowls and cover with some croutons.
2. Sprinkle cheese generously over entire top so sides have some cheese. Broil or bake in a hot oven till cheese melts and bubbles. Enjoy!

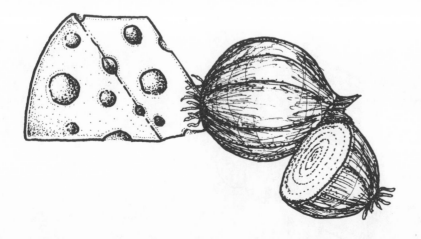

FRUIT "SOUP"

About 2 quarts

This "soup" has many "ethnic" groups that claim it. It can be served warm or cool. It can be used as a meal accompaniment or it's delicious on ice cream or with sponge cake.

1   cup dried apricots
¾   cup dried prunes
3   cups water
2   cups apple juice
¼   cup tapioca
1   cup water
2   cinnamon sticks
4   lemon slices
1   cup sugar
¼   cup raisins
¼   cup currants
1   cooking apple, peeled, cored and sliced

1. In a large saucepan soak apricots and prunes in the 3 cups of water and the apple juice for one hour.
2. While fruit is soaking mix up in a small saucepan the tapioca with 1 cup water. Cook over medium heat until tapioca boils and gets clear. (It will be very thick.)
3. To soaking fruit, mix in cinnamon, lemons, sugar and cooked tapioca. Bring to a boil and *simmer* for 15 to 20 minutes.
4. Stir in raisins, currants and apple slices. Continue to gently simmer until apple slices are just tender—5 to 7 minutes. Stir carefully while cooking but try not to break up fruit.
5. Remove cinnamon sticks if you wish. Serve warm, or when cool.

SALADS

SALAD TIPS

Greens for salads need to be:
    Clean – wash ahead to insure removal of sand and insects
    Cool – prepare hours ahead so they will be chilled.
    Crisp – store properly in plastic bags so greens will be crisp.
Remember to tear greens since cutting bruises them. Dress the
salad at the last minute to insure a crisp tossed mixture.

Fresh fruit salads should have a balance of fruits and color. Don't
overdo by including too many fruits. Make sure you serve the fruit
in luscious size pieces that show off the individual fruit.
An excellent "dressing" to accompany fresh fruit is whipped cream
with fresh or frozen raspberries folded in.

The best way to store leaf lettuce is to wash & dry each piece and place in plastic bags with paper towels. It refrigerates this way for maybe a week and its always ready to use.

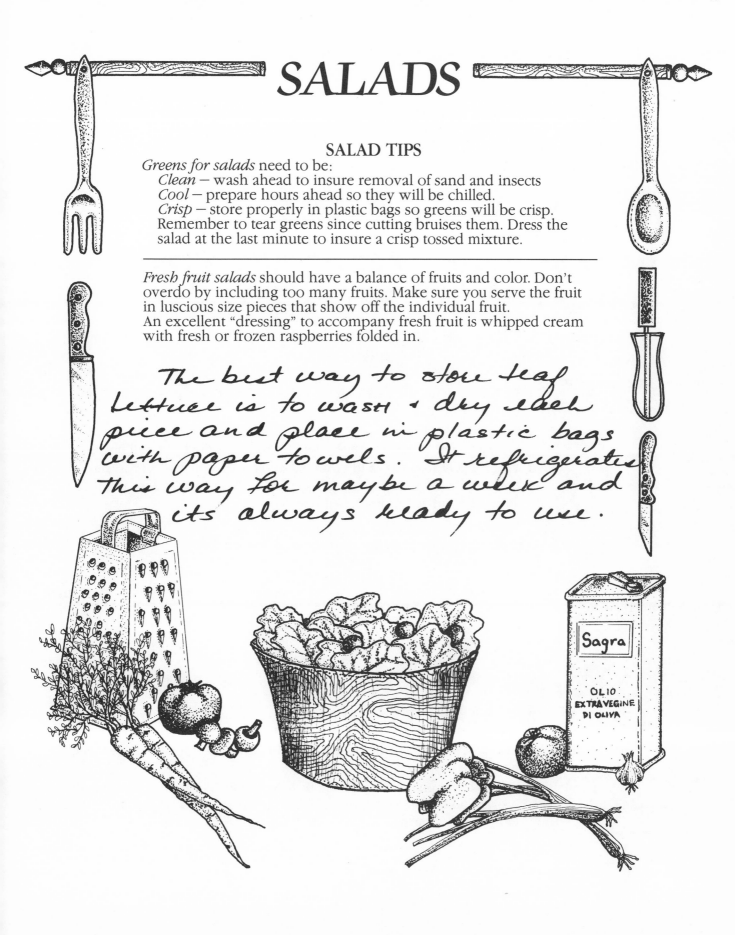

*TIP: Use a blender for the dressing if you have one.

CAESAR SALAD "A LA KARLIN"

Serves 4 — This is my husband's creation and everyone loves it!

1 garlic clove, split
1 small head romaine lettuce, washed and chilled
2 anchovy filets
¼ cup olive oil
1 tablespoon red wine vinegar
1 tablespoon Worcestershire sauce
½ lemon, juice only
1 coddled egg (an egg simmered in the shell for 1 minute)
1 tablespoon Parmesan cheese
  Homemade Croutons
  freshly ground pepper
  Parmesan cheese
  salad bowl

My popular husband has become even more so because of this salad

1. Rub salad bowl well with garlic clove. Tear chilled, crisp lettuce into bowl. Cover and refrigerate.
2. In a bowl mash anchovies and garlic clove together with oil. Beat in vinegar, Worcestershire sauce, lemon juice, coddled egg and cheese.*
3. When ready to serve, add croutons to chilled romaine. Add mixed dressing, freshly ground pepper and more Parmesan cheese if desired. Toss well and serve on chilled plates.

HOMEMADE CROUTONS

WHY BUY croutons WHEN THESE are SO easy & so good

TIP: Use this recipe for French Onion Soup but use olive oil for some of the butter.

Makes about 3 cups

3-4 large slices sour dough bread
4 tablespoons butter or margarine, melted
½ teaspoon garlic powder

Jelly roll pan or flat metal sheet with raised edges

For a nice change — Sprinkle w/ herbs & parmesan cheese.

1. Preheat oven to 450º.
2. Cut up bread into desired sized cubes.
3. In a large bowl toss cubes in melted butter and garlic powder so every cube has some butter on it.
4. Spread cubes on the flat pan and bake for about 10 minutes or until golden brown and crisp. Stir during baking and watch carefully so they don't get too brown or burn.

MARINATED VEGETABLE SALAD

Serves 8

This is great because it can be made ahead. It is good served alone, or tossed on lettuce greens. Use marinade from artichoke hearts with vegetables.

TIP: If you crush dried herbs in your hands before adding them, it helps release the flavors.

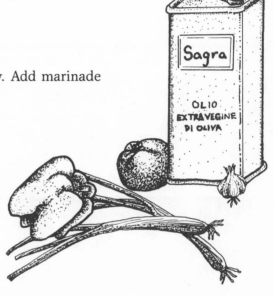

1   *small head of cauliflower, broken up or sliced*
6   *green onions, chopped*
1   *basket cherry tomatoes, halved*
1   *can black olives, drained and sliced*
1   *jar marinated artichoke hearts, cut up*
1   *large green pepper, sliced*
1   *large cucumber, chunked*
3   *stalks of celery, sliced*
    washed lettuce leaves

1. Mix prepared vegetables *except lettuce* together gently. Add marinade and toss.
2. Chill well, tossing every so often.
3. Serve on lettuce leaves or tossed with greens.

MARINADE

½   *cup olive oil*
¼   *cup lemon juice*
1   *teaspoon leaf marjoram*
1   *teaspoon thyme*
½   *teaspoon pepper*
1   *garlic clove, minced*
3   *tablespoons chopped fresh parsley*

1. Mix all ingredients together and add to vegetables to marinate them.

ITALIAN GREEN BEAN SALAD

Serves 3-4

A nice change from regular salad. Use fresh green beans if available. Make ahead if you wish.

1   *package frozen French-style green beans*
1   *tomato, chopped in small pieces*
1   *teaspoon oregano*
½   *red onion, finely sliced*
1   *tablespoon chopped fresh parsley*
3   *tablespoons olive oil*
1   *tablespoon red wine vinegar*
    dash of garlic powder
    salt and pepper

1. Cook green beans until tender-crisp. Drain and chill.
2. Add remaining ingredients and toss with green beans.
3. Serve chilled.

SALAD CHEZ KARLIN

TIP: If you like croutons, use my recipe with Caesar Salad and toss them in at the end.

Serves 6-8

A good combination that is popular. You can vary the ingredients by using marinated artichoke hearts instead of avocado.

1   large head red leaf lettuce
1   (3-4 oz.) chunk of bleu cheese
1   bottle of Bernstein's Italian Dressing
1   large tomato, cut up
1   avocado, cut up
1   small can pitted black olives

1. Wash and chill lettuce.
2. In a small bowl break up bleu cheese with a fork and pour salad dressing over cheese and let sit.
3. Tear up chilled greens in a salad bowl and scatter tomato, avocado and olives around.
4. Immediately before serving, pour on desired amount of dressing and toss lightly.
5. Serve immediately and enjoy.

SINGAPORE CHICKEN SALAD

Serves 4

This mild curry-chutney flavor is a great combination with chicken. Serve on lettuce leaves.

Dressing

¾   cup sour cream
¼   teaspoon salt
½   teaspoon curry powder
1   teaspoon lemon juice
1   tablespoon mango chutney with syrup

1. In a bowl combine dressing ingredients and chill to blend flavors.
2. While dressing is chilling prepare salad ingredients.

Salad

2   large chicken breasts, cooked
1   (8 oz.) can pineapple chunks, or 1 cup fresh,
     if available
1 ½ cups diagonally sliced celery
½   cup toasted slivered almonds
1   cup seedless grapes
     lettuce leaves

1. Shred or chunk cooked chicken and chill if possible.
2. In a mixing bowl gently combine chicken, drained pineapple, celery, almonds, grapes, and chilled dressing.
3. Serve well chilled on lettuce leaves.

CURRIED TUNA RICE SALAD

Serves 6-8

This looks great if molded into a fish shape. Use pieces of vegetables to make the mouth and eyes.

TIP: I'm sure salmon or chicken would be good substitutes.

1   package chicken Rice-a-Roni
1   teaspoon curry powder
½   cup mayonnaise
½   cup sour cream
½   cup sliced celery
½   cup diced green pepper
2   tablespoons minced onion
¼   teaspoon pepper
     salt to taste
1   (7 oz.) can tuna
     orange, pepper, tomato for garnish

1. Cook rice according to package directions. Add curry and cool.
2. Blend mayonnaise with sour cream, celery, green pepper, onion, pepper and salt.
3. Drain and break up tuna.
4. Toss rice with mayonnaise mixture and tuna. Chill completely.
5. Mold and garnish as desired.

SHRIMP SALAD

Serves 4-6

Best if made one day ahead.

TIP: This looks great molded like a fish, using olives for the eyes and mouth.

½   cup raw rice
1   cup water
1   (4½ oz.) can shrimp
½   green pepper
1   small onion
1   small head cauliflower
8   pimiento stuffed olives
     juice of ½ lemon
     dash of tabasco sauce
⅓   cup mayonnaise
     salt and pepper to taste
     olives for garnish

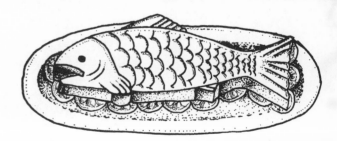

1. In a small covered sauce pan simmer rice in water until tender and all water is absorbed, about 15-20 minutes.
2. Drain and finely chop shrimp.
3. Finely mince green pepper, onion, cauliflower and olives.
4. Combine shrimp, vegetables, rice, lemon juice, tabasco and mayonnaise. Blend well.
5. Salt and pepper to taste. Serve well chilled, garnished with cut olives.

CHINESE CHICKEN SALAD

TIP: If you wish, prepare all the ingredients ahead of time and toss together right before you serve.

Serves 6-8   Much better than restaurants' versions.

2   large chicken breasts
1   small head of iceburg lettuce
2   ounces Mai Fon noodles
    fresh oil for frying
2   tablespoons sugar
1   teaspoon salt
½   teaspoon pepper
3   tablespoons white vinegar
1   tablespoon sesame oil
¼   cup salad oil
2   tablespoons chopped fresh cilantro
5   green onions, chopped
3   tablespoons slivered almonds, toasted*
3   tablespoons sesame seeds, toasted*
    small jar with a lid
    large salad bowl

*Toast almonds and sesame seeds in the oven at 400° until just golden or in a small skillet on low heat. Watch so they don't burn.

1. Cook chicken breasts, strip and chill.
2. In a large salad bowl shred lettuce and chill until crisp.
3. Heat about ½" oil in a skillet and begin frying a few Mai Fon noodles at a time. Oil should be hot enough so when you drop in noodles they should expand immediately. The minute they expand remove and drain on a paper towel. *The noodles should be white—do not let brown.*
4. In a jar combine sugar, salt, pepper, vinegar, sesame oil, salad oil, and cilantro. Shake together until well blended.
5. Toss lettuce, Mai Fon noodles and chicken together. Garnish with green onions, sesame seeds and almonds.
6. Right before you serve, reshake dressing and pour over salad. Enjoy!

BAKED AVOCADO-SEAFOOD SALAD

TIP: Serve one half as a first course or two halves as a main dish.

Serves 4-8   An old favorite.

4   ripe but firm avocados
1   lemon
1   (6 oz.) can small shrimp, drained
1   (6 oz.) can crab, drained and cleaned
¾   cup mayonnaise
2   tablespoons sour cream
3   whole green onions, chopped
¾   cup chopped celery
    Salt and pepper to taste
½   cup crushed potato chips
    Oven safe platter or baking dish

A nice change is to flatten fridge crescent rolls into a pan like a crust. Par bake for 10 minutes. Add seafood salad - Bake 20 minutes & garnish with sliced avocado.

1. Pre-heat oven to 375⁰.
2. Cut avocados in half and remove the seed. Leave halves in the peel.
3. Squeeze a little lemon juice over each avocado half.
4. In a medium bowl combine shrimp, crab, mayonnaise, sour cream, onions and celery. Season to taste.
5. Fill each avocado half with seafood mixture and sprinkle with crushed potato chips. Place on baking sheet.
6. Bake at 375⁰ for 20-30 minutes till mixture is hot.

AUDREY'S POTATO SALAD

Serves 6-8

I got this recipe from my neighbor who brought over some extra salad she had made. My husband likes to mold the salad, and garnish it with paprika and hard cooked eggs.

TIP: Best made a day ahead to let the flavors marry.

6	large white rose potatoes *✱
1	bunch green onions, finely chopped
½	cup parsley, finely chopped
4-5	hard cooked eggs, chopped
	Seasoned salt to taste
	Seasoned pepper to taste
	Best Foods mayonnaise (about two cups)

*Do not substitute russets as they are mushy when cooked—and you need a firm potato.

✱ Red rose potatoes work great - but use 8-9 and don't peel.

Some sour cream or plain yogurt can be used in place of some of the mayonnaise.

1. Peel potatoes and cook in simmering water till tender. Drain well.
2. Cube potatoes into a large bowl.
3. Add green onions, parsley, eggs, salt and pepper. Add mayonnaise and toss until desire consistency. Taste for seasoning.
4. Chill well and garnish.

MUSHROOM SALAD

Serves 4

This is excellent served vinaigrette style over sliced tomatoes or on lettuce leaves.

1	pound fresh mushrooms, sliced
1	cup diced celery
1	cup diced green pepper
2	tablespoons chopped onion
4	tablespoons olive oil
2	tablespoons wine vinegar
½	teaspoon salt
¼	teaspoon ground pepper
4	tablespoons lemon juice
2	tablespoons chopped parsley

1. Combine all ingredients and toss gently. Serve immediately, or let marinate.

WIKI WIKI FRUIT SALAD

TIPS: The steps when combining ingredients should be followed in exact order to prevent the bing cherries from coloring the whole mixture. The whipped cream and the fruit can be prepared ahead and chilled.

Serves 6-8

An excellent combination using fruit that is available year round. Really a dessert but will adapt well to a salad buffet.

1   (16 oz.) can fruit cocktail, drained well
1   (10 oz.) can mandarin oranges, drained well
1   (16 oz.) can pitted bing cherries, drained well and set aside
2   bananas
1   bunch seedless grapes
1   package almonds, sliced
1   tablespoon butter
1   cup whipping cream
1   tablespoon sugar
½   teaspoon vanilla
    ruffled lettuce (garnish)

1. Mix together the well drained fruit cocktail, oranges and grapes and chill thoroughly.
2. Saute almonds in butter till golden. Cool and add to the fruit mixture.
3. In a large bowl, whip the cream and add the sugar and vanilla.
4. Slice the bananas and add to the chilled fruit. Carefully add drained cherries.
5. Gently fold fruit into whipped cream. Mound like a snowball on a plate and garnish with ruffled red leaf lettuce and serve.

PINEAPPLE-CABBAGE SALAD

Serves 4-6

Easy to make—delicious with Mexican food.

1   cup canned pineapple chunks
½   cup raisins
1½   cups cabbage, shredded
2   tablespoons mayonnaise
2   tablespoons sour cream

1. Drain pineapple chunks, reserving 2 tablespoons of juice. Soften raisins in the two tablespoons of juice.
2. Mix together all the ingredients and serve chilled.

HINTS FOR GELATIN MOLDS

1. Never use *fresh* or *frozen* pineapple products as the gelatin won't set up.
2. Run water on the mold and shake out before using.
3. Don't freeze gelatin as it will not hold after being frozen, and any fruit's texture will also be ruined.
4. Molded salads need at least 2-3 hours to set, preferably all day or overnight to really look good.
5. To release salad, dip mold carefully in warm water for 5-10 seconds. Shake to unmold on a plate placed upside down on the mold.

TWO-TONED FRUIT MOLD

Serves 8-10   Beautiful and delicious—well worth the time.

1   *(3 oz.) package black raspberry gelatin*
1   *cup boiling water*
1   *(13½ oz.) can crushed pineapple**
2   *cups blueberries*
1   *(3 oz.) package cream cheese, softened*
1   *(3 oz.) package lemon gelatin*
1   *cup boiling water*
½   *cup cold water*
1   *cup heavy cream*
6   *cup mold*

*Use only canned pineapple in a gelatin mold.

1. In a medium bowl, dissolve black raspberry gelatin in 1 cup boiling water.
2. Drain pineapple, reserving juice. Stir juice into dissolved gelatin.
3. Add blueberries, pour into the mold and chill.
4. Beat together softened cream cheese and lemon gelatin.
5. Add 1 cup boiling water and stir until gelatin is dissolved and cheese is completely blended in.
6. Stir in cold water and chill until the consistency of unbeaten egg whites.
7. Beat chilled lemon mixture until fluffy. Fold in pineapple.
8. Beat cream and fold into pineapple mixture.
9. Spread over firm blueberry layer. Chill until well set.
10. Unmold and garnish as desired.

CUCUMBER RING

TIP: Use red leaf lettuce or dark greens to unmold this beautiful salad on.

Serves 8-10

A fabulous ring mold that is popular and beautiful to serve.

Top Layer

½	envelope unflavored gelatin
½	teaspoon salt
1	tablespoon sugar
¾	cup boiling water
1	tablespoon lemon juice
1	cucumber, unpared and thinly sliced
	6½ cup ring mold

1. In a small bowl mix together gelatin, salt, sugar. Pour in boiling water and lemon juice. Stir well.
2. Overlap cucumber slices in bottom of ring mold. Pour gelatin mixture carefully over cucumbers. Chill till firm.

Second Layer

1	envelope unflavored gelatin
½	teaspoon salt
2	tablespoons sugar
⅔	cup boiling water
¼	cup lemon juice
✱ 6	cucumbers, pared and seeded *(medium)*
8	oz. softened cream cheese
1	cup mayonnaise
¼	cup onion chopped
¼	cup minced parsley
	blender or food processor

1. In a mixing bowl mix together gelatin, salt, sugar, boiling water and lemon juice. Stir well.
2. Puree seeded cucumber slices in a blender or food processor. Drain excess juice.
3. Blend cucumber, cream cheese, mayonnaise, onion, and parsley into gelatin mixture.
4. Pour mixture over first layer and chill.
5. When well set unmold on greens and serve.

✱ When I made this on TV the second layer didn't set properly
Maybe we used too much cucumber or failed to drain them enough.

AUNT HELEN'S STRAWBERRY APPLESAUCE SALAD

Serves 6-8

Very popular—even with "men." This goes nicely with ham or pork roast. I make it in a flat dish and cut "rounds" and serve it on the dinner plate as a garnish.

1   *(3 oz.) package strawberry gelatin*
1   *cup boiling water*
1   *(10 oz.) package frozen strawberries*
1   *cup applesauce*
    8 X 8" flat pan or small mold

1. Dissolve gelatin in boiling water. Add strawberries and stir until thawed.
2. Chill until the consistency of egg whites. Add applesauce and pour into an 8 X 8" pan or small mold.
3. Chill until well set.

TIP: This is beautiful if molded and garnished with sliced kiwi and piped with sour cream for a buffet.

HELEN'S CRANBERRY SALAD

Serves 6-8

This is a popular salad. Delicious with roast chicken or a turkey dinner.

1   *tablespoon unflavored gelatin*
¼   *cup cold water*
1   *(6 oz.) package cherry gelatin*
1   *cup boiling water*
1   *can whole cranberry sauce*
1   *cup sour cream*
1   *4-cup mold*

1. Soften unflavored gelatin in cold water.
2. Dissolve cherry gelatin in boiling water. Mix in softened gelatin and chill until partially set.
3. Add cranberries and sour cream to partially set cherry mixture. Pour into mold or flat pan and chill until set.

TIPS: This takes only a couple of hours to mold but is better if made 8 hours ahead.

ORANGE SHERBERT SALAD

Serves 12   My students love this one. It can be cut in half
easily.

2   (3 oz.) packages orange gelatin
2   cups boiling water
1   pint orange sherbert
2   cups sliced bananas
2   cans mandarin oranges, drained
1   can (1 lb.) crushed pineapple
1   cup cream, whipped
     2-quart mold

1. Dissolve gelatin in boiling water. Add orange sherbert and stir until
   melted. Chill until it reaches the consistency of egg whites.
2. Add drained fruit and fold in whipped cream. Pour into a mold and
   chill until set.

VEGETABLES

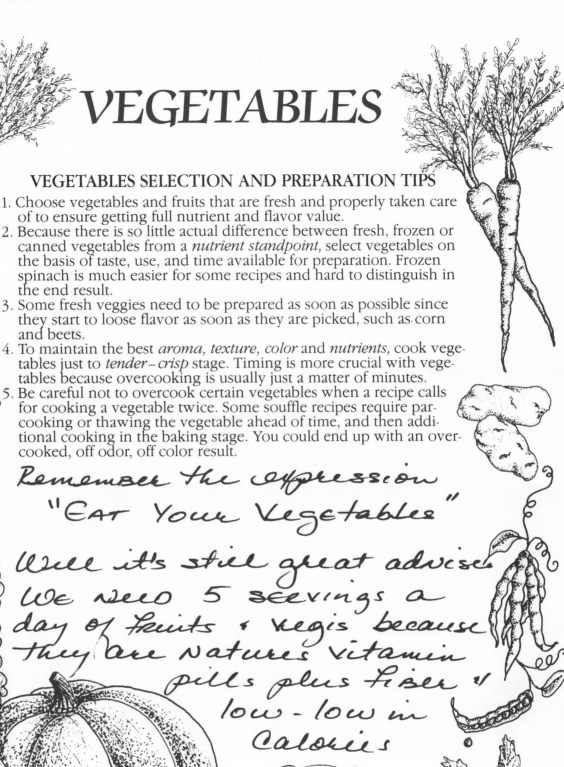

VEGETABLES SELECTION AND PREPARATION TIPS

1. Choose vegetables and fruits that are fresh and properly taken care of to ensure getting full nutrient and flavor value.
2. Because there is so little actual difference between fresh, frozen or canned vegetables from a *nutrient standpoint,* select vegetables on the basis of taste, use, and time available for preparation. Frozen spinach is much easier for some recipes and hard to distinguish in the end result.
3. Some fresh veggies need to be prepared as soon as possible since they start to loose flavor as soon as they are picked, such as corn and beets.
4. To maintain the best *aroma, texture, color* and *nutrients,* cook vegetables just to *tender – crisp* stage. Timing is more crucial with vegetables because overcooking is usually just a matter of minutes.
5. Be careful not to overcook certain vegetables when a recipe calls for cooking a vegetable twice. Some souffle recipes require par-cooking or thawing the vegetable ahead of time, and then additional cooking in the baking stage. You could end up with an over-cooked, off odor, off color result.

Remember the expression
"Eat Your Vegetables"

Well it's still great advice.
We need 5 servings a
day of fruits & vegis because
they are natures vitamin
pills plus fiber &
low - low in
Calories

SPICY BAKED BEANS

Serves 4-6
Delicious and popular with hamburgers or whatever you like beans with. This can be prepared in a microwave—but be sure and cover and do not over cook since the beans could dry out.

½   cup chopped onions
3   slices bacon, cut up
1   (28 oz.) can small pea baked beans
½   cup spicy BBQ sauce
¼   cup brown sugar
1   tablespoon prepared mustard
1½ quart baking dish

My Mom said that the beans burn if you cook them for an hour!

1. Saute onion and bacon in a large frypan for a few minutes.
2. Stir in remaining ingredients and bring to a boil. Simmer over low heat for 5-10 minutes, stirring occasionally.
3. Pour into a greased baking dish and bake in a 400° oven for 1 hour, or *30-45 min* until desired consistency and very bubbly. Watch so that beans do not burn or dry out.

BROCCOLI SUPREME

Serves 8
I think this is one of the most popular broccoli recipes I serve.

2   (10 oz.) packages frozen, chopped broccoli
1   cup creamed cottage cheese
3   eggs
6   tablespoons butter or margarine
⅓   cup flour
½   cup minced onion
1   (8 oz.) can creamed corn
½   lb. cheddar or Swiss cheese, grated
¼   teaspoon salt
¼   teaspoon pepper
    few drops of tabasco sauce
¼   cup soft bread crumbs
3   tablespoons crumbled, cooked bacon (optional)
    2½ quart casserole dish—greased

I wonder if President Bush would eat Broccoli fixed this way?

1. Preheat oven to 350°.
2. Thaw broccoli and drain. (Use a microwave if you have one.)
3. In a large bowl, combine cottage cheese, eggs, 4 tablespoons of the butter, and flour.
4. Fold in broccoli, onion, corn, cheese, salt, pepper, and tabasco. Pour mixture into a greased casserole.
5. Bake at 350° for 1 hour, or until mixture is set.

Read onto the next page to finish the recipe.

6. While mixture is baking, saute bread crumbs in remaining 2 tablespoons butter until just golden.
7. After 30 minutes of baking, sprinkle crumbs and bacon on casserole and continue cooking until mixture is set.

BAKED BROCCOLI

All our grown kids & grandkids love this recipe —

Serves 6-8

This is my oldest son's favorite vegetable dish. Even people who do not like broccoli will eat this.

¼ cup chopped onion
4 tablespoons butter or margarine
2 tablespoons flour
½ cup water
1 (8 oz.) jar Cheez Whiz
2 (10 oz.) packages frozen chopped broccoli, thawed
3 eggs beaten
½ cup soda cracker crumbs
  butter for dotting
  1½ quart baking dish, greased

TIP: It's easy to thaw broccoli right in the package in the microwave. Remove foil wrapping from package if necessary.

1. Preheat oven to 350⁰.
2. In a large pan, saute onions in butter.* Stir in flour and water. Cook and stir until mixture thickens and boils.
3. Add Cheez Whiz, broccoli and eggs. Blend well.
4. Turn into a greased baking dish. Sprinkle soda cracker crumbs on top and dot with butter.
5. Bake at 350⁰ for 45 minutes, or until knife comes out clean.

*Be sure and use a large enough pan to start with so you can make the whole recipe in one pan.

COMPANY BROCCOLI

Serves 6-8

It is easy to prepare and really popular. To change it, add a little curry powder to the sauce.

1 onion, chopped
1 cup sliced celery
½ cup sliced mushrooms
3 tablespoons butter or margarine
2 (10 oz.) packages frozen, chopped broccoli, thawed and drained
1 cup sour cream
1 can cream of mushroom soup
1 cup grated cheddar cheese
1 small package sliced almonds
1 flat or round casserole (approx. 11 X 17")

1. Saute onion, celery and mushroom in butter for a few minutes.
2. Place drained, thawed broccoli in a greased casserole. Layer with sauteed vegetables.
3. Mix sour cream and soup. Spread evenly over vegetables. Sprinkle with grated cheese and almonds.
4. Bake at 350⁰ for 25-30 minutes or until mixture bubbles and broccoli is just cooked.

CAULIFLOWER PARMESAN— *Great Recipe*

TIP: The timing on this recipe is important. Don't beat up the egg whites until the cauliflower is cooked and you are ready to eat.

I promise you that even people who don't like cauliflower will love this!

Serves 6

I learned to "eat and enjoy" cauliflower prepared this way. The topping is excellent on cooked broccoli, too.

1   head cauliflower
2   egg whites
½   cup mayonnaise
¼   cup Parmesan cheese
2   tablespoons chopped parsley
1   tablespoon lemon juice
     Small shallow baking dish or pie plate

1. Cook cauliflower until just tender crisp. Drain and place in the baking dish. Keep warm.
2. Right before serving beat egg whites until fairly stiff. Fold in remaining ingredients and spread over the top of the cooked cauliflower.
3. Broil until topping is set and brown, about 3-5 minutes. Watch carefully! Serve immediately.

GREEN BEANS SUPREME

TIP: Thaw the green beans in the package in the microwave if you have one.

Serves 4

I love this with meatloaf! If you wish, use fresh green beans but par-cook them first.

1   small onion chopped
2   tablespoons butter
1   tablespoon flour
     salt and pepper to taste
½   cup sour cream
1   package frozen French style green beans—thawed
½   cup grated sharp cheddar cheese
     small baking dish

1. In a saucepan, saute onion in melted butter.
2. Mix in flour, salt and pepper and cook until bubbly.
3. Fold in sour cream and beans. Pour mixture into a shallow baking dish.
4. Top with cheese and bake in a 350⁰ oven for 15 minutes or till bubbly.

STIR-FRIED GREEN BEANS

Serves 4   This is spicy "hot" but so good!

4   tablespoons clarified sweet butter (See Tip)
½   cup chopped onions
1   teaspoon finely chopped ginger root
1   teaspoon salt
½   teaspoon pepper
1/8   teaspoon cayenne pepper
1   pound fresh green beans, thinly sliced lengthwise
¼   cup grated coconut
2   tablespoons chopped fresh cilantro*
      dash ground coriander (optional)
2   tablespoons lemon juice
      wok or skillet with a lid

      *Use Italian parsley if cilantro isn't available

TIP: Clarified butter is the clear portion of butter after you have melted it and removed the milky layer. It doesn't burn at high temperatures.

1. In a large skillet or wok heat the butter on medium-high heat.
2. Stir in onions, ginger, salt and pepper while stirring constantly. Add the cayenne and stir-fry for 5 minutes.
3. Drop in the green beans, coconut, cilantro and coriander. Cover and reduce to low heat. Cook stirring occasionally for 10 minutes longer, or until the beans are just tender crisp.
4. Sprinkle with lemon juice and serve.

RATATOUILLE

Serves 8-12   This is good plain, topped with cheese, or as a crepe filling.

2   garlic cloves, minced
1   large onion, sliced
¼   cup olive oil
1   medium eggplant, diced
3   zucchini, sliced
1   green pepper, sliced
1   (28 oz.) can Italian-style tomatoes
1   teaspoon mixed herbs
      salt and pepper to taste
⅓   cup wine (optional)

TIP: This dish tastes better if made ahead. It keeps for a week in the refrigerator.

1. In a deep, large pan saute garlic and onion in oil for a few minutes. Add eggplant, zucchini and green pepper. Toss well and cook for 5 minutes.
2. Add the remaining ingredients and simmer covered for 15-20 minutes.
3. Uncover and finish cooking until desired degree of doneness, about 10-15 minutes.
4. Serve hot or chilled.

EGGPLANT PARMIGIANA

TIP: A 12" non-stick skillet or 12" electric skillet are excellent utensils in which to fry the eggplant.

If you want to avoid the battering & frying just brush the slices with some olive oil & broil them on a cooky sheet until brown on both sides

Continue w/ recipe at step 4

Serves 8-10

This is one of the best ways to get people to eat eggplant. It can be made ahead of time, makes a great buffet dish, and is even good cold.

1   large eggplant
    salt and pepper
2   eggs, beaten
1   cup dry bread crumbs
    cooking oil (some olive oil, if possible)
2   cups of seasoned tomato sauce
    or homemade marinara
1   teaspoon Italian herbs
8   ounces grated mozzarella cheese
¼   cup Parmesan cheese
2   tablespoons finely chopped parsley
    9 X 13" baking dish

1. Wash eggplant and cut crosswise into rounds ⅓" thick. Do not peel. If rounds are very large, cut them in half. Season with salt and pepper.
2. Dip slices into beaten eggs and then into bread crumbs to lightly coat. Place coated slices on a plate and refrigerate for about 30 minutes to set batter.
3. Heat a thin layer of oil in a large skillet and lightly brown the chilled eggplant slices on both sides. Drain on paper towel. Add more oil as needed and continue to brown all the slices.
4. Pour about ¼ of the tomato sauce on the bottom of the greased baking dish. Lay browned slices flat in the baking dish making one layer. Spread some sauce on top of the first layer and sprinkle with a few herbs and some mozzarella cheese.
5. Continue to layer the remaining eggplant on top and pour the rest of the sauce to cover and then sprinkle the remaining herbs on the sauce. Cover with the remaining grated mozzarella and Parmesan cheese.
6. Bake in a 400⁰ oven until mixture really bubbles and eggplant is just tender—about 25 to 30 minutes.
7. Serve sprinkled with parsley.

SAUTEED ONIONS 'N MUSHROOMS

Serves 2

Great on steaks, as a garnish on plain vegetables, or as a basis for hash browns or egg dishes.

2-3 tablespoons olive oil
1   large onion, sliced
4-5 large mushrooms, sliced
    salt and pepper
    large skillet

1. Heat oil in skillet and add onions and mushrooms. Saute on medium high heat until they are as brown and cooked as you like them. Season to taste.

FRANCES' "SURPRISE" CASSEROLE

Serves 8-10   My aunt called it this because it is difficult to guess what is in it. This can be prepared ahead of time and reheats well. If crookneck squash is not available, zucchini works well.

2   pounds yellow crookneck squash, finely cut up or zucchini
½   cup finely chopped onion
½   cup chopped celery
1   cup grated carrots
1   cup sour cream
1   can cream of chicken soup
     seasoned salt and pepper
1   (8 oz.) package herb seasoned stuffing mix (cube type)
1   cube butter or margarine, melted
     9 X 13" baking dish, greased

You might need to cut down on the amount of stuffing since it seems to be too much

1. Cook squash in boiling water until tender crisp. Drain well.
2. Blend the onion, celery, carrots, sour cream and soup into the squash. Season to taste.
3. Toss stuffing in melted butter and pour half of it into the greased baking dish. Spread vegetable mixture over stuffing and top with remaining stuffing.
4. Bake for 35 minutes at 350°, and enjoy.

MOTHER'S FRESH FRIED POTATOES

Serves 4   Try these with BBQ steak or roast beef. The amount will vary with how big the appetites are.

4   large white rose potatoes, scrubbed and sliced very thin
1   bunch chopped green onions (use the whole onion)
     seasoned salt and pepper
     cooking oil
     electric fry pan or 12" non-stick skillet

Unpeeled Red Rose potatoes work great too – but you'll need more

1. Lightly cover the bottom of a large fry pan with oil. Heat to about 350°-400° or use a medium high heat.
2. Layer in the sliced potatoes and onions and season with salt and pepper. Cook 5-10 minutes on one side until they start to brown.
3. Using a spatula, turn them over and continue to brown, turning as needed. Cook to desired degree of doneness. (Mom usually allows about ½ hour to do these.)

CHEESE-POTATO CRISP

Serves 8-10   Like a kugel but with cheese.

2   *large potatoes, peeled and grated*
1   *cup milk*
1   *cup Swiss cheese, grated*
1   *onion, finely chopped*
1   *egg, lightly beaten*
2   *tablespoons melted butter or margarine*
    salt and pepper to taste
    9 X 13" glass dish, well oiled

1. Preheat oven to 375⁰.
2. In a bowl, combine the potato, milk, onion, cheese, egg, and melted butter; season to taste.
3. Transfer to a well oiled flat baking dish.
4. Bake in a preheated oven for 1 to 1½ hours, or until it is very brown and crisp.

POTATOES WITH LEEKS AND CHEESE

Serves 8   Delicious company dish. Best if made ahead.

2   *large leeks*
4   *large russet potatoes, peeled and thinly sliced*
2   *tablespoons butter*
2   *tablespoons flour*
1   *cup chicken broth*
1   *cup milk*
1   *teaspoon seasoned salt*
    freshly ground pepper
1   *teaspoon marjoram*
1   *cup grated Swiss cheese*
3   *tablespoons chopped parsley*
    13 X 9" flat baking dish
    aluminum foil

1. Cut open and wash leeks well. Slice lengthwise and cut into 1" pieces.
2. Grease baking dish and alternate layers of potatoes and leeks.
3. Melt the butter in a saucepan. Stir in flour and cook until bubbly. Blend in broth and milk and continue cooking, stirring constantly, until sauce is thick and smooth.
4. Blend in remaining ingredients and pour on top of potatoes and leeks.
5. Cover with foil and bake in a 350⁰ oven for 1 hour or more until the potatoes are soft to a fork test. Remove foil near the end to brown top if desired.

"SWEET POTATO" SOUFFLE

Serves 6-8

A real favorite at holidays because it is not too sweet. It can be made ahead and refrigerated till ready to bake.

3   yams (sweet potatoes are too dry)
¼   cup butter
1   egg
1   tablespoon brandy or sherry
    salt
    pepper
    nutmeg
    butter for dotting
1½ quart casserole

TIP: You can bake this while the gravy is being made and the turkey is being sliced.

1. Bake yams at 450⁰ until soft—about one hour.
2. Scoop out baked yams and mash up with butter.
3. Add egg, brandy, salt and pepper to taste, and *beat* until light and fluffy.
4. Pour into a greased casserole. Sprinkle with nutmeg and dot with some butter.
5. Bake at 350⁰ for about 20-30 minutes until hot and puffy.

HERB SPINACH BAKE

Serves 6

This is great for a buffet because it holds well.

1   (10 oz.) package frozen chopped spinach, thawed
1   cup cooked rice
1   cup grated cheddar or swiss cheese
2   eggs, slightly beaten
½   cup milk
¼   cup chopped onion
2   tablespoons soft butter
½   teaspoon Worcestershire sauce
¼   teaspoon salt
¼   teaspoon rosemary or thyme leaves, crushed
    8 x 8" baking dish

TIP: Be sure you use 1 cup of fully cooked rice rather than uncooked rice.

1. Thaw spinach and drain.
2. Mix spinach with remaining ingredients and blend well.
3. Pour mixture into a flat greased baking dish.
4. Bake in a 350⁰ oven for 25 minutes or until mixture is set.

CREAMED SPINACH

TIP: Try par-cooking the spinach in the microwave in the package.

Serves 3-4

A must with roast beef and yorkshire pudding. This can be made ahead and reheated.

1   *package frozen chopped spinach, par-cooked*
3   *tablespoons butter*
2   *tablespoons chopped onion*
3   *tablespoons flour*
1   *cup milk*
    dash nutmeg
    Lawry's seasoning salt & pepper
    garlic powder

1. Melt butter in a saucepan. Blend in onion and flour. Heat until bubbly.
2. Blend in milk. Cook on medium heat stirring continually until the sauce is thick and boiling.
3. Add drained par-cooked spinach to sauce and mix well.
4. Season to taste and reheat till mixture is very hot.
5. Serve with a pat of butter in the center of the spinach.

SPECIAL VERSION OF CREAMED SPINACH

1   *package frozen chopped spinach, par-cooked*
2   *pieces of bacon, chopped*
3   *tablespoons chopped onion*
3   *tablespoons butter*
4   *mushrooms, sliced*
3   *tablespoons flour*
1   *cup milk*
    dash nutmeg
    Lawry's seasoning salt & pepper
    garlic powder
    dash of mixed herbs

1. In a large skillet saute onion in bacon until bacon cooks a little. Add butter and saute mushrooms in mixture for a few minutes.
2. Blend in flour and milk and cook until sauce thickens and boils.
3. Stir in par-cooked spinach and season to taste.
4. Serve hot.

BAKED SPINACH FONDUE

Serves 6

Delicious alone but beautiful when baked inside a scooped out tomato.

TIP: This holds better than a souffle but should not be over baked.

4 eggs, separated
1 (10 oz.) package frozen, chopped spinach, thawed
3 cups small, fresh bread cubes
1 can Cream of Mushroom soup
1 cup grated Jack cheese
¼ teaspoon Worcestershire sauce
seasoned salt
garlic powder
pepper
2 quart baking dish

Forget the salt & Worcestershire since the soup is salty enough.

1. Preheat oven to 350⁰.
2. Beat egg yolks. Blend in spinach, bread, undiluted soup, cheese and seasonings to taste.
3. Beat egg whites until just stiff and fold together with spinach mixture.
4. Pour into greased baking dish and bake for 50-60 minutes, or until a knife comes out clean.

SAUTEED VEGETABLES

Serves 4-6

This mixture is delicious alone, topped with cheese, served over pasta or as a crepe filling.

1 bunch of green onions
1 onion, sliced
½ lb. mushrooms, sliced
1 green pepper, stripped
1 red pepper, stripped
1 tomato in small chunks
2 garlic cloves, minced
2 tablespoons chopped parsley
¼ cup olive oil
1 teaspoon Italian herbs
salt and pepper
1 cup grated Swiss or fresh Parmesan cheese

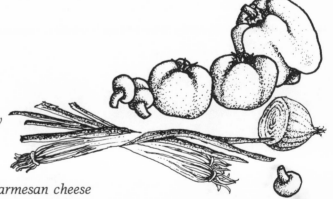

1. Wash and chop up *entire* green onions in 1″ pieces. Prepare remainder of vegetables. Set aside.
2. In a large skillet on high heat, add olive oil. Immediately add garlic and onions and saute for a minute.
3. Add mushrooms, peppers, parsley, and herbs. Toss well and saute till vegetables are just tender.
4. Add tomato and season to taste.
5. Serve topped with cheese, if desired.

STUFFED ZUCCHINI

Serves 8

I created this recipe in an attempt to recreate a dish I had at someone's home.

4 large, thick zucchini
¼ cup chopped onion
1 cup finely chopped mushrooms
1 clove garlic, minced
3 tablespoons butter
¼ teaspoon thyme
¼ cup soft bread crumbs
   seasoned salt and pepper
2 tablespoons Parmesan cheese
1 egg, beaten
½ cup Jack cheese, grated

1. Cut zucchini in half lengthwise.
2. Par-cook zucchini in simmering water about 5 minutes.
3. Cool slightly and carefully scoop out pulp, leaving a nice firm shell. Chop pulp and set aside.
4. Saute onions, mushrooms and garlic in butter.
5. Mix sauteed mixture with thyme, bread crumbs, Parmesan cheese, egg and half the pulp of the zucchini. Season to taste with salt and pepper.
6. Fill zucchini shells with mixture and place in a greased baking dish. Top with grated cheese.
7. Bake in 400⁰ oven until hot and cheese is bubbly, approximately 20 minutes.

ZUCCHINI "SOUFFLE"

Serves 6-8

Easy to make and the flavors of cheddar cheese and fresh garlic make this dish special.

3 lbs. zucchini, sliced
12 Ritz crackers, crushed
1 garlic clove, minced
3 eggs, beaten
⅓ cup oil
½ lb. grated sharp cheddar cheese
   salt and pepper to taste
   1-2 quart casserole

1. Preheat oven to 350⁰.
2. Cook, drain and mash zucchini.
3. Combine all ingredients with zucchini and mix very well.
4. Pour into greased casserole and bake at 350⁰ for about 40 minutes, or until firm.

EGGS & CHEESE ENTREES

GENERAL EGG TIPS

Eggs are an incredible foodstuff, but they must be handled correctly to get the right results.

1. Always use *large eggs* in recipes. Since eggs add moisture, color, flavor and fat, changing the size will affect many factors in the final product.
2. Separate eggs when they are cold.
3. Beat up or add eggs to mixtures when they are at room temperature because they blend and extend better.
4. Cook on medium to low heat and never boil eggs because it toughens the protein and creates rubbery egg whites.
5. Don't overcook, because it causes curdling or syneresis which causes quiches or egg dishes to weep.
6. Always add warm mixtures into eggs to prevent scrambling eggs.

Unfortunately the cholesterol scare has caused many people to give up eating eggs.

Too bad since they are such a valuable source of protein, vitamins and minerals.

REMEMBER that balance & variety is the KEY to a good diet. Limit your egg intake to 4-7 per week unless your doctor advises you otherwise.

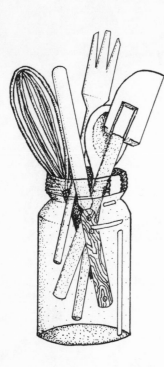

SOUFFLE AND EGG BEATING TIPS

1. Clean bowls and beaters are essential with egg white foams. They will not beat up in the presence of any fat (i.e. egg yolks).
2. When separating a number of eggs use three bowls to prevent accidents. One small glass bowl to collect each individual white and a second bowl for all the yolks. Then the third bowl is the beating bowl where you place each white that is separated (that way no accidents occur by ruining your batch of whites).
3. Use only metal or glass bowls for beating whites. Copper bowls are best since the acid in copper stabilizes whites.
4. Separate eggs when cold and beat at room temperature.
5. Wire whips will incorporate more air or volume in whites but power mixers are necessary for longer beating jobs such as meringues.
6. Beat whites just to stiff peak stage where the whites still tip over but are not dry.

BROCCOLI SOUFFLE

Serves 4-6

This souffle holds pretty well and is best with the creamy mushroom sauce.

1   (10 oz.) package frozen chopped broccoli
    (thawed and drained)
4   tablespoons butter (½ cube)
¼   cup sifted flour
½   teaspoon salt
1   cup milk
1   cup grated cheddar cheese
4   eggs, separated*
    1½ quart souffle dish
    beating bowl and wire whip*

*See tips on souffles and eggs.

1. Preheat oven to 350⁰.
2. Thaw broccoli in the microwave if possible and drain thoroughly. Finely chop broccoli.
3. In a saucepan, melt butter, stir in flour and salt. Add milk and cook and stir over medium heat until mixture thickens and bubbles. Remove from heat.
4. Stir in cheese until melted, then the thawed broccoli.
5. In a medium bowl, beat egg yolks until light yellow. Blend in broccoli mixture until thoroughly mixed.
6. In a *clean* beating bowl (metal or glass), beat egg whites with wire whip until fairly stiff but not dry.
7. Gently pour broccoli mixture over egg whites, folding together until well blended.
8. Pour into ungreased souffle dish. Bake in preheated 350⁰ oven for 35-40 minutes, or until a knife inserted on the side comes out clean. Serve immediately with Creamy Mushroom Sauce.

CREAMY MUSHROOM SAUCE

Makes 1½ cups   Easy sauce to make and delicious on lots of things but particularly souffles.

TIP: Make sauce while souffle bakes or make ahead and add sour cream at the end and reheat.

¼ *cup chopped onions (green or white)*
2 *tablespoons butter*
1 *tablespoon all-purpose flour*
½ *cup light cream or milk*
1 *(3 oz.) can sliced mushrooms, drained*
¼ *teaspoon salt*
¼ *teaspoon pepper*
½ *cup dairy sour cream*

1. In a small saucepan, saute onions in butter for a minute. Stir in flour.
2. Add cream, mushrooms, salt and pepper. Heat to boiling, stirring constantly.
3. Stir in sour cream and gently heat. *Do not allow mixture to boil or sour cream will curdle.*

DOUBLE CHEESE SOUFFLE

TIP: This souffle will get a nice "top hat" if you run a spatula around the edge of the souffle dish right before you bake it. A copper bowl will make a real difference with this souffle.

Serves 6-8

This souffle is dynamite and just beautiful. Make sure people are ready to eat when it comes out of the oven because this souffle won't hold. Be sure to make the sauce with it because it is a nice complement.

⅓ cup butter
⅓ cup sifted flour
½ teaspoon salt
1/8 teaspoon pepper
    heavy dash of nutmeg
1½ cups milk
6 egg yolks, well beaten
¾ cup Swiss cheese, grated
¾ cup Parmesan cheese
6 egg whites*
¼ teaspoon cream of tartar
2 tablespoons Parmesan cheese, for top
2½ quart souffle dish
beating bowl with wire whip*

*See tips on souffles and eggs.

1. Preheat oven to 350⁰.
2. Melt butter in a saucepan. Stir in flour, salt, pepper and nutmeg. Cook over medium heat, stirring constantly, until mixture bubbles.
3. Stir in milk slowly and continue to cook and stir constantly until mixture bubbles and thickens.
4. Remove milk mixture from heat and stir in Swiss and ¾ cup Parmesan cheeses.
5. Mix some cheese sauce into well beaten yolks to warm yolks.*
6. Return warmed yolk mixture to the remainder of the sauce and blend well.
7. In a deep, clean bowl, metal or glass, beat egg whites and cream of tartar with a wire whip. Continue to beat until mixture is fairly stiff, but not dry.*
8. Add a little beaten egg white to the cheese mixture and then gently fold cheese sauce into egg whites. *Fold* until fairly well blended, being careful not to overmix and knock air out of the whites.
9. Pour mixture into souffle dish and sprinkle with 2 tablespoons Parmesan cheese. Bake at 350⁰ for 45 to 50 minutes, until a knife inserted in the side pulls out clean. *Serve immediately* with Tomato-Mushroom Sauce, if desired.

HERB TOMATO-MUSHROOM SAUCE

This can be made while souffle bakes. It keeps well.

½   pound mushrooms, sliced
3   tablespoons butter or margarine
2   tablespoons flour
1   teaspoon sugar
¼   teaspoon salt
1/8 teaspoon pepper
½   teaspoon basil or Italian herbs
2   cups tomato juice
3   tablespoons parsley, chopped

1. In a saucepan, saute mushrooms in butter.
2. Blend in flour, sugar, salt, pepper and basil. Cook on medium heat, stirring until mixture bubbles.
3. Slowly stir in tomato juice and continue to cook and stir until mixture begins to thicken and boil. Add parsley and serve when souffle is ready.

QUICK CHEESE 'N HERB SOUFFLE

Serves 4

This is easy because you use cream of mushroom soup as the sauce base. Vary the cheese and use crab or chicken if you like.

1   (10 oz.) can cream of mushroom soup
¾   cup grated cheddar cheese
3   tablespoons Parmesan cheese
¼   cup minced green onion
1-2 tablespoons minced parsley
4   eggs separated
¼   teaspoon cream of tartar
     2 quart souffle dish
     beating bowl and wire whip*

     *See tips on souffles and eggs.

1. Preheat oven to 350⁰.
2. In a medium saucepan, mix together soup, cheese, onions, and parsley. Heat and stir over medium heat until cheese begins to melt. Remove from heat.
3. In a mixing bowl, beat egg yolks until light yellow and then gradually blend soup mixture into beaten yolks.**
4. In a clean beating bowl (metal or glass) beat egg whites and cream of tartar with a wire whip until fairly stiff, but not dry.
5. Gently fold cheese sauce into beaten whites. Pour mixture into a souffle dish.
6. Bake in a 350⁰ oven for 45-50 minutes, or until a knife inserted on the side comes out clean. Serve immediately.

**Blend in crab at this point. *or a can of tuna or salmon can be used.*

TUNA SOUFFLE

TIP: Be sure to blend tuna into egg yolks, and not the reverse.

Serves 3-4

A fancy way to use tuna, or substitute crab if you like. Good with the creamy dill or mushroom sauce.

¼ cup butter or margarine
¼ cup sifted flour
½ teaspoon salt
1/8 teaspoon pepper
3 tablespoons chopped onion
1 cup milk
¼ cup Swiss cheese, grated
1 (7 oz.) can tuna, drained
4 egg yolks, well beaten
5 egg whites*
  1½ quart souffle dish
  beating bowl with wire whip*

*See tips on souffles and eggs.

1. Preheat oven to 350°.
2. Melt butter in a saucepan. Stir in flour, salt, pepper and onion. Cook over medium heat, stirring constantly, until mixture bubbles.
3. While constantly stirring, blend in milk. Cook over medium heat, continuing to stir until sauce thickens and boils. Remove from heat and add cheese and tuna, blending until cheese melts. Cool slightly.
4. In a bowl beat the egg yolks well and blend the warm tuna mixture slowly into the yolks.
5. In a *clean* beating bowl (metal or glass), beat egg whites with wire whip until fairly stiff but not dry.*
6. Gently *fold* sauce into egg whites. Pour mixture into a 1½ quart souffle dish. Bake in a 350° oven for 50-55 minutes or until knife inserted on the side comes out clean.
7. Serve immediately.

CREAMY DILL SAUCE

2 tablespoons butter or margarine
3 tablespoons chopped onion
1 (3 oz.) can mushrooms,
  or 4 fresh sliced mushrooms
2 tablespoons all purpose flour
¼ teaspoon dill
¼ teaspoon salt
  pepper
1¼ cups milk

1. In a saucepan, brown onion and mushrooms in butter. Stir in flour and seasonings.
2. Add milk and cook and stir on medium heat until mixture thickens and boils.

SPINACH SOUFFLE

Serves 4

This must be served immediately, so have everyone ready when you remove it from the oven.

TIP: Don't use the same beaters for the egg yolks and whites.

- 5 tablespoons butter
- ¼ cup chopped onion
- ¼ pound chopped mushrooms
- ¼ cup sifted flour
- 1 cup milk
- 4 eggs, separated*
- ½ package frozen chopped spinach (thawed and drained)
- ½ teaspoon seasoned salt
  dash of nutmeg
- 1/8 teaspoon garlic powder
  pepper to taste
- ¼ teaspoon cream of tartar
  1½ quart souffle dish
  beating bowl and wire whip*

*See tips on souffles and eggs.

1. Preheat oven to 350⁰.
2. In a large saucepan, saute onion and mushrooms in melted butter. Blend in flour. Add milk and cook on medium heat, stirring constantly, until mixture is thick and boiling. Cool slightly.
3. In a good sized mixing bowl, beat egg yolks until light yellow. Add spinach, salt, nutmeg, garlic and pepper. Fold in milk sauce.
4. In a *clean* beating bowl (metal or glass) beat egg whites and the cream of tartar with the wire whip until farily stiff but not dry.*
5. Carefully fold sauce into beaten whites until fairly well blended.
6. Pour mixture into a lightly greased 1½ quart souffle or deep casserole dish.
7. Bake in a 350⁰ oven for 50-60 minutes or until a knife inserted on the side comes out clean.

The Microwave works fine but because you have to bake the crust 1st I think that its easiest to do the whole procedure in the regular oven.

QUICHE SUGGESTIONS

1. Glass or ceramic pie pans are best to help absorb heat and cook the pastry and prevent soggy crusts.
2. Chill the crust well before you fill it.
3. Use an unpricked crust and don't fill it until oven is preheated and you are ready to bake.
4. Having cold ingredients—milk, eggs, at *room temperature* increases blending ability and decreases cooking time.
5. Quiches are egg custards. To test for doneness of mixture, insert knife 1" off center. If knife comes out clean, it's done. Remove from oven and let set up before slicing. Do not overcook as toughening of the protein and weeping will occur.

QUICHE LORRAINE

Gewurztraminer or Riesling   Serves 6-8

This is pretty much a standard quiche with some nice seasonings.

Real men do eat Quiche

1	9" chilled, unbaked pie shell in a glass pie plate*
8	bacon slices
4	thin slices boiled ham, diced
1	small onion, chopped
2	cups (8 oz.) grated Swiss cheese
3	eggs, room temperature
1	cup heavy cream
½	cup milk
¼	teaspoon salt
¼	teaspoon pepper
¼	teaspoon dry mustard
1/8	teaspoon "Bon Appetite" or "Beau-Monde" seasoning
	dash of nutmeg
	dash of cayenne pepper

*See quiche or pastry tips

1. Preheat oven to 425⁰.
2. In a skillet cook the bacon crisp. Crumble and set aside.
3. Drain the skillet and then saute the ham and onion for a few minutes.
4. Sprinkle the bacon, ham and onion over the bottom of the prepared pie shell. Cover evenly with grated cheese.
5. Beat the eggs with cream, milk and all the seasonings. Pour mixture over the cheese in the pie shell.
6. Bake in a 425⁰ oven for 30-45 minutes, or until mixture is firm and a knife comes clean one inch from the center. (If the quiche gets too brown turn the oven down to 375⁰ and continue cooking until done.)
7. Let stand for 10 to 15 minutes before serving so quiche can finish setting up and will be easier to slice.

"JONI'S" SPECIAL QUICHE

Serves 6-8

This was a result of a number of recipes we had created at school. Joan Robinson, one of my former students, really deserves credit as she made it for 75 persons at a faculty luncheon. Try it, you'll love it—everyone does.

1	9" chilled, unbaked pie shell in a glass pie plate*
2	bacon slices
1	onion, chopped
1	cup chopped mushrooms
½	cup chopped celery
2	tablespoons chopped green pepper
1	garlic clove, minced
1	zucchini, parcooked, chopped and drained
1	tomato, peeled, seeded and chopped
3	eggs, room temperature
¾	cup milk
½	teaspoon mixed herbs
¼	teaspoon each, seasoned salt and seasoned pepper
1	tablespoon chopped fresh parsley
¼	cup grated Parmesan cheese
1½	cups grated Swiss cheese

*See quiche and pastry tips

1. Preheat oven to 425º.
2. In a large skillet cook the bacon crisp. Remove bacon, crumble and set aside. Reserve fat in the skillet.
3. In the same skillet with the drippings, saute onions, mushrooms, celery, pepper and garlic for a few minutes. Mix in *drained*, parcooked zucchini and prepared tomato. Cook a minute on high until most of the liquid is reduced. Drain excess if necessary.
4. In a large mixing bowl, beat eggs with milk and seasonings. Stir in cheeses and then mix in sauteed vegetables and crumbled bacon.
5. Pour mixture into chilled unbaked pastry shell. Bake in preheated 425º oven for 30-45 minutes or until mixture is firm and a knife comes clean one inch from the center.*
6. Let stand 10 to 15 minutes before serving so quiche can finish setting up and will be easier to slice.

*Peeling and seeding tomatoes reduces excess moisture & bitterness

Ask Robin - my TV food assistant about peeling & seeding 8 tomatoes on her 1st day on the job.

CHICKEN, VEGETABLE QUICHE

Chardonnay or Fume Blanc   Serves 6-7   This has mushrooms, onions and spinach in it to make it tasty.

1   9" chilled, unbaked pie shell in a glass pie plate*
1   (10½ oz.) package frozen chopped spinach
¼   pound mushrooms, sliced
6-8 green onions, chopped
1   tablespoon butter
1   cup cooked chicken, shredded
1   cup Swiss cheese, grated
3   eggs
1¼   cups light cream (half and half)
½   teaspoon seasoned salt
1/8 teaspoon dried tarragon

See quiche and pastry tips

1. Preheat oven to 425⁰.
2. Defrost and squeeze dry chopped spinach.
3. Saute mushrooms and onions in butter for a few minutes and then layer chicken, mushrooms, onions and cheese in a prepared pastry shell.
4. In a medium bowl, beat eggs, cream, salt, and tarragon until well blended. Blend in defrosted spinach. Mix well.
5. Pour egg blend over mixture in pie shell. Bake at 425⁰ for 30-45 minutes or until mixture is firm and a knife comes clean.* (If the quiche gets too brown, turn the oven down to 375⁰ and continue cooking until done.)
6. Let stand 10 to 15 minutes before serving so quiche can finish setting up and will be easier to slice.

SAUSAGE, SPINACH AND CHEESE PIE

Rose or Beaujolais   Serves 8   This pie is really an attractive super main dish. The filling would be great in small appetizer turnovers or baked in crepes or pasta shells.

1   9" glass pie plate
     pastry for double crust (see pies)
1   pound Italian sausage
6   eggs
2   (10 oz.) packages frozen, chopped spinach, (thawed and drained)
1   pound mozzarella cheese, grated
⅔   cup ricotta cheese
1   teaspoon salt
1/8 teaspoon pepper
1/8 teaspoon garlic powder
1   tablespoon water (for egg wash)
     pastry brush

1. Make pastry and wrap in plastic wrap and set aside.
2. Remove sausage from casings and break up in a skillet, and stir sausage until brown—about 10 minutes. Drain off any fat that accumulates.
3. Set aside one egg yolk for an egg wash. In a large bowl, combine remaining 5½ eggs with thawed spinach, cheeses and seasonings. Blend in browned sausage and set aside.
4. Preheat oven to 375⁰.
5. Divide prepared pastry into two pieces. Roll out as directed for a double crust recipe.
6. After top crust is rolled out, spoon filling into bottom crust. Cut a small circle in the center of the top crust and arrange over filling. Seal and flute edges and decorate pie top with rerolled pastry scraps. Cut some vent holes in the top crust.
7. Take reserved egg yolk and mix with 1 tablespoon water to make an egg wash. Brush the top of the pie with the egg wash. Bake in a preheated 375⁰ oven for 1 hour and 15 minutes, or until pie is golden.
8. Let pie stand 10 minutes and then cut into desired serving pieces.

CREPES

12-15 crepes

These take a little practice to get the technique down pat. Use this recipe for all your main dish and dessert crepes. You can double this recipe. They refrigerate for days and freeze well.

TIP: Use a blender or food processor for the batter if you want.

The blender makes the hour standing period really unnecessary.

2   eggs
1   cup milk
½   teaspoon salt
1   cup flour
2   tablespoons melted butter
     melted butter for pan
     crepe pan or small non-stick 6" skillet

1. In a mixing bowl, beat the eggs well with a wire whip.
2. Beat in milk, salt, flour and butter until smooth.
3. Cover batter and let stand in the refrigerator for an hour.
4. Heat the pan on medium high and brush with a little butter.
5. Ladle several tablespoons of batter in pan and tilt pan around until batter coats pan evenly in a thin layer. Pour extra batter back into bowl, if necessary.
6. Cook for a few minutes until underside just begins to brown. Carefully flip crepe over for a minute or so and then turn out on a plate. (Don't flip crepe over if you want to cook one side only.)
7. Repeat until all batter is used. *If your pan is seasoned you won't need to keep brushing with butter.*
8. Stack crepes on top of each other. Fill as desired or refrigerate or freeze, well wrapped.

CHICKEN AND ARTICHOKE CREPES

Blush wine, or fruity white wine. 4 cups

This filling is great in crepes, patti shells or over pasta.

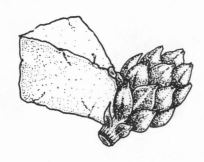

4	tablespoons butter
¼	pound sliced mushrooms
3	tablespoons flour
1	cup milk
½	cup chicken broth
½	cup grated Swiss cheese
¼	cup Parmesan cheese
1	teaspoon Worchestershire sauce
1	(8 oz.) package frozen artichoke hearts, cooked and drained
1	cup cooked chicken, shredded
2	tablespoons sherry or white wine
	seasoned salt and white pepper
	flat casserole for service
	grated cheese for topping

1. In a medium saucepan, saute mushrooms in butter. Stir in flour.
2. Gradually blend in milk and broth and cook on medium heat until thick and bubbly. Remove from heat and stir in cheese.
3. Stir in Worcestershire sauce, artichoke hearts, chicken, wine, and season to taste.
4. Fill crepes as desired. Sprinkle with some grated cheese.
5. Heat in a 300º oven until warm.

Ham variation:
   To vary recipe, add 1 cup of ham in place of artichoke hearts.

Topping for Crepes:

This finishes the crepes nicely. Broil the topping for a few minutes, if you can.

1	cup white sauce
¼	cup mayonnaise
¼	cup Parmesan cheese
1-2	tablespoons white wine
1	tablespoon minced parsley

In a small bowl
1. Beat the 5 ingredients together.
2. Put some sauce on each crepe before heating for service.

✱ Barbara Siegel my lab tech at Santa Monica College really created this recipe for an event we had.
Sorry Barb - that I didn't give you more credit & thanks for all your help.

CHEESE BAKE

Serves 6-8

Great for a crowd—delicious as a brunch dish with fresh fruit or as a meatless main dish. This dish holds well and is good cold but it tends to sink when it cools.

TIP: If you have a can of crab available, add this with the cheese before the milk and eggs are poured on top.

6 eggs
1 cup milk
½ cup flour
1 teaspoon baking powder
1 cup cottage cheese
1/8 teaspoon seasoned salt
1 cube butter, cut up in small pieces
1 pound Jack cheese, cubed
1 (3 oz.) package cream cheese, cut up
   seasoned pepper
   parsley and green onions for garnish
   13 X 9" glass baking dish

1. Preheat oven to 350⁰.
2. In a large mixing bowl, beat the eggs and milk together. Continue to beat in the flour, baking powder, cottage cheese and salt till well blended.
3. Evenly dot or distribute the butter, cubed cheese and cream cheese over the bottom of the baking dish. (See Tip.)
4. Pour the egg and milk mixture all over the butter and cheese. Sprinkle lightly with some seasoned pepper.
5. Bake at 350⁰ for one hour or until mixture is set and is somewhat brown on top. Serve warm and garnish if desired with chopped parsley and green onion.

GRITS "SOUFFLE"

Serves 4-6

Most Californians don't appreciate grits until they taste this and it opens a whole new world—this is usually served as a side dish but it makes a great main dish with a salad on the side. It's easy to do because the eggs aren't separated.

TIP: This may be made ahead of time, adding the eggs just before baking.

3 cups milk
¾ cup quick cooking grits
6 tablespoons butter, cut up
1 teaspoon salt
1/8 teaspoon cayenne pepper
2 cups grated Swiss or cheddar cheese
4 eggs, well beaten*
   greased 2 quart casserole or souffle dish

   *See souffle tips.

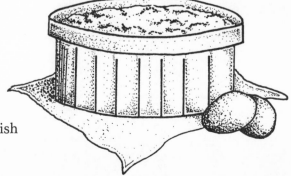

1. Pre-heat oven to 350º.
2. In a saucepan, bring milk to a simmer and stir in grits.
3. Reduce heat and continue to stir until it becomes a thick mush—about 5-7 minutes. Remove from heat.
4. Add butter, salt, cayenne pepper and cheese, beating in well with a wooden spoon.
5. Beat in eggs and pour into the well-buttered casserole or souffle dish.
6. Bake uncovered, for 1 hour and 10 minutes or until well-puffed, golden brown and set up.

OVEN CHEESE STRATA

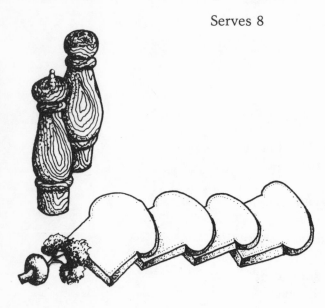

Serves 8

These dishes are also called Fondues, because of the bread. You can vary the ingredients and the Strata can be made ahead or the night before.

8   slices of firm bread
4   eggs, beaten
2½   cups milk
1   (10 oz.) can cream of mushroom soup
2   tablespoons Vermouth or white wine
¼   cup onion, chopped
2   tablespoons minced parsley
¼   teaspoon pepper
½   teaspoon dry mustard
1   cup chopped Polish sausage*
2   cups grated cheddar or Swiss cheese
     large casserole dish, greased

*Use ham, salmon, tuna or chicken in place of sausage.

1. Remove crusts from bread and cut bread into cubes.
2. In a large bowl, beat eggs, milk, soup, wine, onions, parsley, mustard and pepper together.
3. Fold in bread, sausage and cheese and pour mixture into greased casserole dish.
4. Refrigerate for an hour if you can, or overnight, well wrapped.
5. Bake at 325º for one hour, or until strata is firm and a knife pulls clean.

PASTA, GRAINS & CASSEROLES

HOW TO COOK PASTA

1. Buy a good brand – either imported or high in semolina. "You get what you pay for!"
2. Use lots of water – slightly salted and one tablespoon of oil added. Bring to a rolling boil.
3. Add spaghetti and boil on the highest heat possible so it is moving constantly.
4. Cook till al-denté (to the bite) not raw or mushy.
5. Drain and serve. Don't rinse unless necessary.

PASTA WITH SHRIMP AND VEGETABLES

Rose, or light Italian red or Zinfandel

Serves 4-6

This is probably my most popular creation, particulary with my students. The timing is important *so have all the ingredients prepared ahead*, and then do the veggies first. While the spaghetti is cooking, saute the shrimp.

Sauteed Vegetables

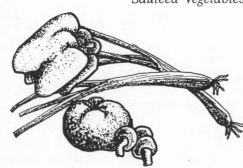

½   cube butter
3   tablespoons olive oil
2   green peppers, thinly sliced
1   large onion, sliced
1   bunch green onions, cut in 1″ pieces
¾   pound mushrooms, sliced
2   teaspoons Italian herbs
1   large tomato, diced
¼   cup Vermouth
     salt and freshly ground pepper
     large skillet or large sauce pan

1. In the large skillet, melt butter on high heat. Add oil and when hot, add peppers, onions and mushrooms. Saute on medium high for 4 or 5 minutes, stirring regularly.
2. Add herbs, tomato, Vermouth and season with salt and pepper.
3. Let simmer for a few minutes, gently mixing vegetables to blend. Set aside.

Shrimp

1   pound raw shrimp, cleaned, butterflied
     with tail piece intact
½   cube butter
4   tablespoons olive oil
3   tablespoons minced parsley
3-4 garlic cloves, minced
½   lemon, juiced
¼   cup Vermouth
     large skillet

1. In the large skillet, melt butter on high heat and add olive oil.
2. When hot (not smoking) add shrimp, parsley and garlic. Saute until shrimp turn opaque.
3. Immediately add lemon juice and wine and let mixture boil for a minute or so, to reduce sauce.
4. Pour shrimp and sauce into the sauteed veggies and blend carefully so that the seasonings mix well. Keep warm.

Presentation

> 1   *pound spaghetti, cooked al dente*
> 1   *(approx. 4 oz.) chunk of fresh Parmesan cheese, grated like regular cheese*
> 2   *tablespoons minced parsley for garnish*
>   *large platter or dinner plates*

1. Place cooked, drained spaghetti on the platter, or give each "plate" a portion.
2. Pour entire shrimp mixture and vegetables over pasta. Sprinkle grated cheese and parsley over entire dish. (Or, serve a portion of sauteed shrimp and vegetables on each plate and sprinkle with cheese and parsley.) "So-o-o-o good!"

"SUPER" SPAGHETTI CASSEROLE

Serves 4-6

This combination is a real winner. My husband will eat it all if I don't hide the leftovers. It can be made ahead. Just bake before serving.

> 3   *tablespoons butter or margarine*
> 1   *clove garlic, minced*
> 1   *large onion, sliced*
> ½   *pound mushrooms, sliced*
> 2   *(10½ oz.) cans cream of celery soup*
> ¼   *cup milk*
> ¼   *cup dry sherry or white wine*
> 1   *cup grated cheddar or Jack cheese*
> 2   *(6½ oz.) cans tuna, drained*
> 1   *small can black olives, sliced*
> 1½   *teaspoons chili powder*
>   *seasoned salt and pepper*
> ⅓   *cup chopped parsley*
> ½   *pound spaghetti, broken in 6" pieces*
> 2-3   *tablespoons Parmesan cheese*
>   *2½ quart greased casserole*

1. Cook spaghetti al dente and drain. Set aside. (See Tip.)
2. In a skillet saute garlic, onion and mushrooms in butter till slightly brown. Put in a large mixing bowl.
3. Blend in soup, milk, wine, ½ cup cheese, tuna, olives, seasonings, and parsley.
4. Fold in cooked spaghetti and pour into a greased 2½ quart casserole. Top with remaining ½ cup cheese and Parmesan cheese.
5. Bake in 375⁰ oven until cheese is melted and somewhat brown—about 30 minutes.

TIP: Al dente means "to the bite," which is properly cooked pasta.

Young robust red, California "Burgundy,"

BOB'S SPAGHETTI

TIP: This freezes well and will refrigerate for a week. A *stainless steel* kettle is best for tomato-based mixtures since it doesn't corrode if you need to store the sauce in the cooking pan.

Zinfandel, Chianti

3-4 quarts

This is by far my husband's best recipe. My mother has always been fond of Bob but I really think she's in love with his spaghetti sauce because he makes it for her when we go to Laguna. Serve with meatballs and Italian sausage, too, if you like.

	large kettle with lid (see Tip)
⅓	*cup olive oil*
½	*bunch parsley, chopped*
2	*onions, chopped*
3-4	*large garlic cloves, chopped*
1	*large bell pepper, chopped*
3-4	*celery stalks, chopped*
½	*pound mushrooms, sliced*
1	*round tablespoon Italian herbs*
2	*teaspoons seasoned salt*
½	*teaspoon pepper*
1	*(12 oz.) can tomato paste*
2	*(15 oz.) cans tomato sauce*
1	*(26 oz.) can tomatoes*
1	*teaspoon crushed hot red chilies*
½	*cup wine*
	sugar
	Meatballs
	spaghetti
	Parmesan cheese
	sauteed Italian sausage links (if desired)

1. Heat oil in the kettle and add all prepared raw vegetables. Sprinkle with herbs, salt and pepper and saute for 5 minutes.
2. While veggies are gently sauteeing, prepare meatballs and place on top of cooking vegetables. Cover mixture and let "simmer" for 5-7 minutes.
3. Add all the tomatoes, chilies and wine and mix gently to blend but *try not to break up meatballs.* Cover
4. Gently heat mixture on medium to low heat just to a gentle simmer— stirring occasionally. *Watch so bottom doesn't stick and burn.*
5. Continue to simmer for 2 to 3 hours. Adjust seasoning and add more wine and some sugar if sauce seems too tart.
6. Serve over al dente (to the bite) spaghetti with meatballs and sausage. Pass the cheese and as Bob says, "You should enjoy."

MEATBALLS

Optional if you want a meatless sauce, but Bob insists on these for flavor, too.

1½ pounds lean ground beef
1   egg
1   teaspoon Italian seasoning
¼   teaspoon garlic powder
      salt and pepper

1. In a bowl, mix meat, egg and seasonings.
2. Make very firm 2″ balls and add to sauce as directed.

SOUTHERN CALIFORNIA BAKE

Serves 6-8   The combination of flavors is terrific. This can be made ahead a few days and refrigerated. It is good left over.

Dry rose, Zinfandel

1   pound ground beef
⅓   cup chopped green onion
½   pound sliced mushrooms
2   zucchini, sliced
1   large clove garlic, minced
1   teaspoon salt
2   teaspoons chili powder
1   (7 oz.) can diced green chiles
2   cups cooked rice
1   cup sour cream
2   cups grated cheddar or Jack cheese
2   large tomatoes, sliced
      seasoned pepper
      green chili salsa (optional)
      9 X 13″ greased baking dish

1. In a large skillet, saute ground beef until it just loses its pinkness. Set meat aside in a large bowl.
2. In the same skillet, lightly brown the onion, mushrooms, zucchini and garlic. (Use a little oil if necessary.)
3. To the meat, add the sauteed vegetables, salt, chili powder, chilies, cooked rice, sour cream and one cup of the cheese. Mix well.
4. Pour into the greased baking dish and cover with one layer of sliced tomatoes. Top with the remaining cup of cheese. Sprinkle with seasoned pepper for color.
5. Bake at 350⁰ for 30 to 40 minutes or until hot. Serve and pass the green chili salsa, if desired.

PAELLA

Rose, Spanish red, young red or Zinfandel.

Serves 6-8

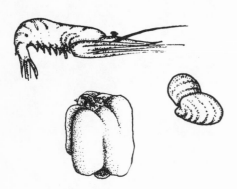

This Spanish dish has always intrigued me but I wasn't satisfied with restaurant versions. I think this is quite good—hope you like it as much as the Karlin household does. You can vary the ingredients—sausage, fish, etc.—according to your preference. I'd serve Paella with a salad or a fruit dish. If you can, let people see what it looks like from the oven, then serve individual portions, giving people the variety they prefer.

salt and pepper
3 *tablespoons olive oil*
1 *whole chicken, cut up*
¼ *cup water*
1 *teaspoon oregano or mixed herbs*
3 *tablespoons chopped parsley*
2 *large onions, sliced*
2 *garlic cloves, minced*
½ *pound mushrooms, sliced*
1 *green pepper, sliced*
1 *red pepper, sliced*
1 *large tomato, chopped*
3 *tablespoons butter or margarine*
2 *cups uncooked rice*
1/8 *teaspoon ground saffron*
3 *cups chicken broth*
1 *cup white wine*
4 *Italian sausages, or preferred sausage*
1 *pound medium shrimp, cleaned, with tails intact*
  oil for sauteeing
1 *lobster, cleaned and cooked*
1-2 *dozen clams in the shell, scrubbed*
  large skillet with lid
  Paella pan
  or oven proof skillet-shaped casserole dish

1. Wash, dry and season chicken with salt and pepper. In the large skillet brown chicken pieces well in olive oil.

2. Add water, herbs, and parsley, then cover. Simmer on low heat until the chicken is just cooked—10-15 minutes.

3. Remove cooked chicken from the skillet and set aside. To the juices in the same skillet add the onions, garlic, mushrooms, peppers and tomato. Saute until the vegetables are slightly tender.

4. In a large saucepan melt the 3 tablespoons of butter and add the rice. Stir constantly. Add the saffron, broth and wine and bring to a boil. Cover and gently simmer until rice is tender—20-25 minutes. *Do not use Minute Rice.*

5. While the rice is cooking prepare the rest of the ingredients you plan to add—since only the clams will actually *cook* in the oven. Saute the sausage till just done and slice in thick chunks.

6. Saute the shrimp and lobster in the sausage juice (and oil if needed) until it just loses its clearness. Cut up the lobster in chunks, still in the shell.

7. Now mix the cooked rice and sauteed vegetables with any juice together. Taste for seasonings. Gently mix in chicken pieces and sausage.

8. Preheat oven to 400°.

9. Grease the large serving casserole—*it must be ovenproof*—and put in the rice and chicken mixture. Carefully add fish pieces into rice and place uncooked clams all around on the casserole.

10. Bake mixture in the 400° oven until everything is hot and clams have opened. Serve with pride!

CAROL LEE'S VEGETABLE-RICE

Serves 4

This can be a main dish for non-meat eaters or a wonderful side dish with roast beef, chicken or ham.

1   *cup chopped green onions*
½   *cup sliced celery*
½   *cup chopped green pepper*
1   *garlic clove, minced*
2   *tablespoons butter*
2   *cups hot cooked rice*
2   *tomatoes, chopped*
1   *cup cheddar or Jack cheese, grated*
¼   *cup chopped parsley*
¼   *teaspoon seasoned salt*
½   *teaspoon Worcestershire sauce*
2   *tablespoons Parmesan cheese*
     casserole dish

1. Saute green onions, celery, green pepper and garlic in butter for a few minutes.

2. In a large bowl add sauteed vegetables to hot rice, tomatoes, cheese, parsley and seasonings. Mix gently so cheese begins to melt. Taste for seasonings.

3. Pour rice mixture into a greased serving, oven-proof dish. Sprinkle with some Parmesan cheese and keep warm until time to serve. (If you need to hold, cover so mixture will not dry out.)

CHICKEN "CON QUESO"

Blush wine, or fruity white wine.

Serves 8-10

Delicious main dish especially popular for brunch or luncheon guests. The chicken and vegetables can be made ahead of time, if desired.

6   *chicken breasts*
    seasoned salt and pepper
2   *(13 oz.) cans chicken broth or equivalent*
2   *onions, chopped*
1   *cup celery, sliced*
2   *carrots, sliced*
2   *tablespoons butter*
⅓   *pound mushrooms, sliced*
    9" or 10" square casserole or equivalent

1. Wash and dry chicken breasts. Season with salt and pepper and place in a large saucepan or dutch oven.
2. Add the chicken broth, and half of the onion, celery and carrots. Cover and bring to a boil. Simmer about 15-20 minutes or until the chicken is cooked.
3. While the chicken is cooking, saute the remaining vegetables in 2 tablespoons butter for a few minutes. Set aside.
4. When chicken is cooked, remove from the broth and when cool enough to handle, shred meat from bones. Discard the skin and bones.
5. Strain broth and reserve 1⅓ cup for the sauce. Save the vegetables and extra broth.

Sauce

⅓   *cup butter*
½   *cup flour*
1⅓ *cup reserved broth*
1   *cup cream*
1   *cup Jack cheese, grated*
    salt and pepper

1. Melt the butter in a saucepan over medium heat. Stir in the flour and blend in the broth and cream. Continue to cook, stirring constantly, until sauce thickens and boils.
2. Remove from heat and stir in cheese until melted. Season to taste. Adjust thickness, if necessary, with broth.

Biscuits

2   *cups biscuit mix*
½   *cup milk*
3   *ounces cream cheese*
2   *tablespoons milk*
1   *tablespoon chives, chopped*
1   *tablespoon parsley, chopped*

1. Combine biscuit mix and milk until a dough forms. Knead on a flat surface for a minute until somewhat smooth. Roll out into an 8" square.
2. Beat cream cheese, milk and herbs together. Spread dough with this cheese mixture.
3. Roll up jelly-roll fashion. Cut roll into 10-12 slices.

Assembly

1. Preheat oven to 425º.
2. Cover the bottom of the square deep casserole with the shredded chicken.
3. Arrange vegetables on the top and then pour the prepared sauce over the chicken and vegetables.
4. Place the sliced biscuits—cut side up—on top. Bake at 425º for 25 minutes or until biscuits are cooked and brown and sauce mixture is bubbly and hot throughout.

JOE'S SPECIAL

Serves 3-4   A quick nutritional dinner and great left over. Just serve sliced tomatoes and cucumbers and sour dough bread with it.

Young Zinfandel, Beaujolais

1 garlic clove, minced
1 onion, chopped
¼ pound mushrooms, sliced
1 tablespoon olive oil
1 pound lean ground beef
1 (10 oz.) package frozen chopped spinach, thawed and drained
1 teaspoon mixed herbs (or basil, oregano, marjoram) seasoned salt and pepper
5-6 eggs, beaten
   Parmesan cheese

1. In a large skillet, brown garlic, onion and mushrooms in oil. Add beef and continue browning for a few minutes.
2. Stir in thawed spinach and herbs. Season to taste. Continue to saute until spinach is slightly cooked and mixture is well blended.
3. Add beaten eggs and stir mixture on *medium heat* until eggs are set and mixture just holds together.
4. Serve hot, sprinkled with Parmesan cheese.

TALI-SARI

Beaujolais, Zinfandel,
Red Rhone or Italian red

Serves 8-10

An easy casserole that I forget about and then when I serve it, everybody raves, especially my son Jeff. You can vary seasonings to your taste. Delicious as a left-over or cold.

Ground turkey will work fine in almost any dish calling for ground beef.

2	minced garlic cloves
1	cup chopped onion
1	large green pepper, chopped
2	pounds ground beef
1	(8 oz.) package wide noodles, cooked and drained
1	can cream of mushroom soup
1	(1 lb.) can corn
1	(1 lb.) can tomatoes, cut up
1	teaspoon prepared mustard
2	teaspoons Worcestershire sauce
1	teaspoon paprika
½	teaspoon salt
¼	teaspoon Tabasco sauce
½	cup chopped parsley
1	cup grated cheese
	seasoned pepper (optional)
	2-3 quart baking dish

1. In a large sauce pan, saute garlic, onion, pepper, and ground meat on high heat until just brown.
2. Add cooked noodles and the rest of the ingredients except cheese and seasoned pepper. Mix gently but thoroughly and taste for seasonings.
3. Pour into a greased large baking dish. Cover with foil and bake at 375⁰ for 30 minutes or until hot.
4. Uncover and top with cheese and garnish with some seasoned pepper. Continue to bake until cheese melts and mixture is bubbly.

STUFFED EGGPLANT "A LA KARLIN"

Zinfandel, Beaujolais,
Italian red wine

Serves 4

I love the stuffed eggplant at La Grange restaurant. This is not exactly the same but it's a nice variation.

2	medium eggplants
1	pound ground veal or beef
1	large onion, chopped
2	garlic cloves, minced
¾	pound fresh mushrooms, chopped
	salt and pepper
¼	teaspoon thyme leaves
1	large tomato, finely chopped
1	egg, beaten
2	cups Mozzarella or Jack cheese, grated

1. Cut eggplants in half lengthwise and salt. Let stand 15 minutes.
2. Saute veal, onion, garlic, and mushrooms on high heat 5 to 7 minutes. Add seasonings to taste.
3. Saute eggplant *flat side down* until par-cooked, 5 to 8 minutes. Scoop out pulp of eggplant, leaving a firm shell.
4. Chop up pulp and add about 1 cup to the veal mixture. Add tomato and egg and mix well. Taste for seasoning.
5. Fill shells with mixture. Top with cheese.
6. Bake in a 375⁰ oven until filling is hot—about 25-30 minutes. Enjoy.

TAMALE PIE

Serves 6-8

This is delicious even if you don't like tamales. A green salad, warm tortillas and fruit are perfect with it.

TIP: Better if made ahead, and this freezes well, too.

1   large onion, chopped
1½ pounds ground beef
    garlic salt
    chili powder
4   tamales, cut up
1   (28 oz.) can whole tomatoes
1   (8 oz.) can tomato sauce
1   can pitted black olives
1   (16 oz.) can of corn
    or (10 oz.) package frozen corn
3   tablespoons fresh, chopped parsley
2   cups grated Jack or cheddar cheese
    green chile salsa
    black olives
    chopped green onion
    13 X 9" or large flat baking dish

My dear Friend Bev Haas wants to know what size can of olives.
My reply "How many olives do you like?"

1. Brown onion and meat together in a skillet. Season well with garlic salt and chili powder. Pour into a large mixing bowl.
2. Add cut tamales, tomatoes, tomato sauce, olives, corn and parsley to the meat mixture. Mix well and pour into a greased flat baking dish.
3. Top with grated cheese and bake at 400⁰ till hot and bubbly, about 30-40 minutes.
4. Serve accompanied with black olives, chili salsa and chopped green onion for people to garnish as desired.

BEEF TORTILLA CASSEROLE

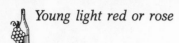 *Young light red or rose*

Serves 4-6

Using ground meat makes this quick, although cooked chicken and turkey work well. My friends and family from the East Coast really like this "kind" of Mexican food.

1   pound ground meat
1   onion, chopped
    seasoned salt and pepper
    garlic powder
1   can cream of mushroom soup
1   (4 oz.) can green chili salsa
8   corn tortillas—cut into 1 inch strips
2   cups grated Jack or cheddar cheese
    chopped green onions and green chili salsa
    flat baking dish

1. In a skillet, brown meat and onion. Season to taste.
2. Mix soup with salsa.
3. Grease the baking dish and then place half of the stripped tortillas on the bottom of the dish. Cover the tortillas with half of the meat mixture, then half of the soup mixture, and one cup of the cheese.
4. Repeat the layer once, ending with the cheese. Bake at 350⁰ for 30-45 minutes or until bubbly. Let sit for 5-10 minutes before serving, to set up.
5. Serve and garnish with chopped green onions and chili salsa, if desired.

RICE PILAF

Serves 4-6

Usually served as a nice side dish with grilled meats, poultry or seafood. Add some sauteed mushrooms to this, if desired.

¼   cup butter (½ cube)
1   cup long grain rice
4   green onions, chopped
¼   cup broken up thin spaghetti (1" pieces)
2½ cups stock and water combination
    salt and pepper
    covered saucepan

1. Melt the butter in the saucepan and add the rice, onions and broken up spaghetti. Saute for a few minutes to lightly brown mixture, stirring constantly.
2. Add stock and water to pan and simmer on low heat covered until rice is cooked, about 20-25 minutes. Taste for seasonings.

SEAFOOD

SEAFOOD TIPS

My husband Bob loves to fish and I love to cook and eat it. This would seem to indicate good compatibility since he recently caught over 100 pounds of fish in Alaska. The problem is that every time I suggest cooking the fish from our overstuffed freezer, he says he is not in the mood for fish.

1. The best guide for seafood selection, other than catching it fresh yourself, is to deal with a *reliable* fish merchant who offers the best quality available.
2. *Remember* to keep seafood on ice in your refrigerator until you prepare it–not more than a day or two. If it is fresh, you may freeze it if necessary.
3. Seafood has very little fat or connective tissue so it needs only to be cooked until it loses its clearness. If you cook it until it flakes, it is probably overdone.
4. Some "fish" is already cooked, e.g., lobsters and crabs, and just need to be heated. Be careful not to toughen them by cooking too much.

Clams & mussels need to be soaked ahead of time so they will release their sand.

If they fail to open up after a reasonable amount of cooking time — Don't Eat Them!

HERB BROILED FISH

Use the sauce to brush on grilled fish or poultry

TIP: Remember not to turn the fish. Just turn broiler off to hold fish. If fish is too thick to broil, just bake at 425⁰ until done.

French Muscadet and Sauvignon Blanc.

I like to add more green onion & parsley even some mushrooms around the fish while it broils — it gives you more brown degis in the sauce.

Add more wine at the end to make more sauce if needed.

Serves 2-3

Easy and even fish haters like it this way. Extra sauce can be made if desired, and ingredients can easily be varied.

1   pound fresh fillet of fish (sole, salmon, halibut)
1   tablespoon butter
1   tablespoon olive oil
    juice of ½ lemon
3   whole green onions, chopped
1   garlic clove, minced
1-2 tablespoons sherry or sweet wine *or dry vermouth*
    seasoned salt and pepper
¼   teaspoon mixed herbs
2   tablespoons chopped parsley
1-2 tablespoons Parmesan cheese
    lemon wedges
    chopped parsley
    bottom of broiler pan

1. In a sauce pan, melt butter, add oil, lemon juice, onions, garlic, sherry, salt and pepper to taste, and mixed herbs.
2. Place fish on a greased broiler *bottom* pan and pour sauce over fish. Sprinkle with chopped parsley and Parmesan cheese.
3. Broil 3 inches from heat and baste every few minutes with sauce that is around fish. Continue broiling on same side until fish is brown and it just loses its clearness. *If it flakes easily it is too done.*
4. Serve fish on warm plates and pour any drippings over it. Garnish with chopped parsley and lemon wedges.

CRAB IMPERIAL

TIP: If used as a stuffing in fish, put crab into uncooked seafood and bake or broil till seafood is done and crab is hot.

Chardonnay

Serves 2-3
or stuffing for 4

This is best made with Virginia blue crab meat, but good snow crab or canned crab works well. This mixture may be baked alone in a small casserole or be used as a stuffing for lobster, trout or in cooked artichokes.

1   pound crab meat or 2 (6 oz.) cans
    well drained fancy crab meat
⅔   cup mayonnaise
1   tablespoon Dijon mustard
    or 2 tablespoons Durkee's sandwich sauce
¼   teaspoon Old Bay Seasoning* (optional)
    salt and pepper
    soft bread crumbs from 2 bread slices
    Parmesan cheese

*Available in seafood markets.

1. Drain crab meat.
2. In a medium bowl, beat mayonnaise, mustard and seasonings. Fold in crab and bread crumbs until well mixed.
3. Spoon into small casserole and sprinkle with Parmesan cheese.
4. Bake at 450⁰ until hot and brown, about 10-15 minutes.

"SCAMPI" ✳

Serves 3-4

Scampi, or shrimp, is prepared in the usual method with garlic and lemon. You can vary this by adding some chopped tomato and different herbs. Serve with pasta or rice and a green vegetable.

Fume Blanc, Chardonnay, or French Muscadet

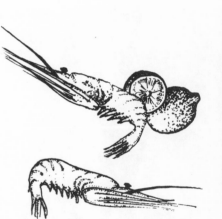

✳ Melt butter & mix with rest of the ingredients & then use as a marinate

1	pound medium to large shrimp, cleaned and butterflied but with tail intact
½	cube butter
2	tablespoons olive oil
3	tablespoons minced parsley
3	garlic cloves, minced
1-2	tablespoons lemon juice
2-3	tablespoons sweet wine or Vermouth
	salt and pepper
1	tablespoon minced parsley for garnish
	large 12" skillet

1. Prepare shrimp and wash and dry on paper towels and keep cold until ready.
2. In skillet, melt butter on high heat and add oil, parsley and garlic. (Watch that it does not smoke or burn.)
3. When mixture is sizzling hot, add shrimp into skillet and keep them separated, if possible. Saute for a minute or so on each side or until shrimp turn opaque.
4. As soon as shrimp start to cook, add lemon juice and wine and stir mixture together.
5. Let sauce boil for a minute or so to reduce liquid. Add more wine if needed.
6. Serve scampi immediately with sauce and garnish with parsley.

✳ I've discovered this recipe adapts well to a BBQ or broiler.
Just use ingredients as a marinate for shrimp or skewered fish kabobs & brush seafood w/ mixture as you grill them.

Shrimp — on a hot fire take just a minute or two on each side or broil until brown.

BAKED STUFFED FISH

Fume Blanc or Light Chardonnay

Serves 4

You can use a thick piece of fish, two filets or the ideal way is to use a whole fish and stuff the inside.

1   *small salmon or thick piece of fish*
1   *cube butter or margarine*
⅓   *cup celery, chopped*
¼   *cup green onions, chopped*
2   *tablespoons parsley, minced*
3-4 *mushrooms, chopped*
1½ *cups dried seasoned bread cubes
      (Pepperidge Farms or similar)
      salt and pepper*
½   *cup butter and wine (for basting)
      lemon wedges
      oiled flat baking pan (bottom of broiler pan)*

1. Wash and dry fish.
2. Preheat oven to 400⁰.
3. In a large skillet melt butter and saute celery, onion, parsley and mushrooms, for a few minutes.
4. Stir in bread crumbs and season to taste. Add a little water or wine to moisten if needed.
5. Stuff fish and close with toothpicks, if necessary (or make a slash in thick fish and stuff).
6. Place fish on oiled baking pan and brush with butter and wine mixture. Place any extra stuffing around fish and baste.
7. Bake in 400⁰ preheated oven until fish loses its "clearness" at thickest part. Baste every 5 or 7 minutes. Do not overcook, but be sure to cook fish throughout.
8. Cut fish so everyone gets a piece with stuffing. Serve with lemon wedges and any pan drippings if possible.

CIOPPINO

Serves 4

A delicious Italian style fish stew that originated in San Francisco. You can vary the seasonings and the fish according to your taste. Because it is expensive, fix it only for those who really will appreciate it. If you have a tureen, take it full to the table and let people serve themselves.

TIP: The sauce can be made ahead and then reheat and add the fish right before serving.

Light Italian red, young Zinfandel or spicy young Cabernet

1	*8-quart deep saucepot with lid*
¼	*cup olive oil*
1	*onion, chopped*
1	*bunch of green onions, chopped*
3	*garlic cloves, minced*
1	*green pepper, chopped*
2	*celery stalks, chopped*
6	*mushrooms, chopped*
2	*cups chicken stock*
1	*bottle clam juice*
1	*cup dry wine*
2	*tablespoons sherry, marsala, or sweet Vermouth*
1	*(28 oz.) can Italian tomatoes*
1	*(8 oz.) can stewed tomatoes*
1	*or 2 (8 oz.) cans tomato sauce*
½	*teaspoon basil*
½	*teaspoon leaf thyme*
½	*teaspoon leaf oregano*
¼	*cup chopped fresh parsley*
1	*bay leaf*
	dried red pepper to taste (1/8 teaspoon)
	salt and pepper
1	*pound firm white fish, chunked*
1	*pound raw whole medium shrimp*
1	*cup (½ pint) scallops*
1	*dozen clams—in shells*
	lobster and crab—cut up in shells
	large soup bowls
	crusty French bread
	empty bowl for shells

1. Heat the olive oil in the large pan and saute the onions, garlic, pepper, celery, and mushrooms in the oil for 5 minutes.

2. Add the remaining ingredients except the seafood and simmer for 30 minutes. Taste and adjust seasonings. Add more liquid if necessary. (Mixture should resemble a marinara sauce.)

3. Add any of the raw fish, shrimp and scallops and simmer covered in the sauce until the fish just begins to turn white and the clams start to open up (7-10 minutes). Immediately add any cooked fish (*lobster and crab—in the shells*) and heat until the cooked fish is hot. *Don't over cook or you will toughen the fish..*

4. Dish up portions in large soup bowls and serve with crusty French bread.

QUICK SEAFOOD SOUP

Young light red or rose   Serves 3-4

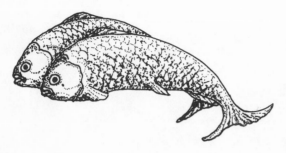

This is so easy to fix but tasty and a good way to get your vegetables. Use any fish of your choice. Serve with steamed rice.

3   tablespoons olive oil
1   onion, chopped
2   garlic cloves, minced
1   green pepper, chopped
¼   cup parsley, minced
2   large mushrooms, chopped
3   green onions, chopped (optional)
1   teaspoon mixed herbs (of your choice)
¼   teaspoon crushed red chiles or pepper
      dash of saffron
1   (8 oz.) bottle of clam juice
1   (8 oz.) can of stewed tomatoes
1   cup semi-sweet wine (Vermouth)
1-2 pounds meaty white fish
      cleaned clams and shrimp (optional)
      stuffed olives for garnish
      deep skillet or sauce pan

1. In a large deep skillet, heat olive oil and saute chopped vegetables for a few minutes.
2. Add remaining ingredients *except fish*, and simmer for 5 to 10 minutes. Taste for seasoning. Add more liquid, if needed (broth or wine).
3. About 15 minutes before serving, add desired seafood to simmering sauce. When fish starts to cook, turn in sauce and continue to cook until fish turns white and clams open.
4. Serve fish with rice and plenty of sauce. Garnish with olives.

MEAT

MEAT SELECTION AND PREPARATION TIPS

You should include small amounts of meat in your diet regularly, if possible, because it is an excellent source of iron, B vitamins and protein.

Modern methods of raising meat have produced leaner, more tender animals. Older selection and preparation techniques should be adjusted for newer recommendations.

1. Select your meat cut according to use and method of cooking desired. If you want to barbeque a steak, buy a cut that will lend to that method best, e.g., top sirloin, New York or filet.

2. Always calculate the amount of bone and fat to estimate the amount of servings – *very lean, boneless meat will yield* 2-3 servings per pound. *High percentage of bone and fat,* will require 1 to 2 pounds per serving.

3. Meat may be cooked with dry or moist heat, but the method selected should be according to the *cut, amount of fat and leanness.* Lean, tender cuts of beef, veal or lamb are best if served rare to medium in doneness, to maintain tenderness and juiciness. Overcooking many cuts will make them dry and tough. (If you cook round of beef or liver well done, with no moisture, it could turn out like shoe leather.)

4. Pork needs to be cooked to at least 140° (rare) to kill the trichinosis. Most people prefer their pork cooked more well done.

5. When roasting meat or poultry, use a shallow pan and a rack to elevate the meat. This will allow air to circulate around it. *Do not cover* or add much moisture.

6. Roast meat at 325 to 350° and use a meat thermometer to determine accurate doneness. The temperature of the meat and the thickness of the muscle will determine the cooking time.

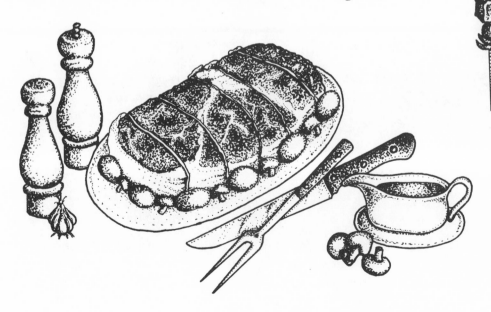

MY LOVE AFFAIR WITH HAMBURGER

TIP: The best buy for ground meat is to buy a round steak, have it trimmed and ground.
California burgundy or Zinfandel

Add a little good mustard if you like

Serves 1

If you know me at all you know that I like hamburger any way I can get it. Just ask Grace Berry about the time I ordered beef tartar for lunch at L'Ermitage.

I created a version that is a nice change from the bun, lettuce, pickle version. This is good with a baked potato, sauteed onions and a salad.

⅓ to ½ pound extra lean ground beef (see Tip)
1 tablespoon onion, finely chopped
3-4 pimiento stuffed olives, chopped
1 tablespoon mayonnaise
pepper to taste
1 tablespoon grated cheese

1. In a bowl, mix meat and the rest of the ingredients, so meat holds together.
2. Make a firm patty.
3. On high heat saute or BBQ very fast so meat is very brown but still pink on the inside—a few minutes on each side.
4. Serve and enjoy.

COUNTRY MEATLOAF *Ground turkey products work just fine.*

TIP: Never taste a mixture that has raw pork in it.
Young robust red, California "Burgundy," Zinfandel

In the Microwave: Use glass utensil cook until meat is at least 150° or medium well. 20-30 minutes

Serves 4-6

I threw this together one night and my "family" thinks it's great. I like this served with green beans, fresh corn and small browned potatoes.

2 pounds lean ground beef
1 pound bulk pork sausage
1 large onion, chopped
3 tablespoons parsley, chopped
2 garlic cloves, minced
1 teaspoon mixed herbs (optional)
2 eggs
¼ cup bread crumbs or oatmeal — *more oatmeal might be needed*
¼ cup BBQ sauce
¼ teaspoon pepper
¼ teaspoon salt
13 X 9" baking dish

1. In a large bowl, place ground meats. Add the remaining ingredients and mix well with your hands until mixture is well blended.
2. Form two loaves, approximately 9 X 5" each, and place them into baking dish, parallel to each other but so they do not touch.
3. Bake at 375° for about 1 hour or until meat is at least 150° or medium doneness and browned.
4. Serve hot or cold.

BEEF 'N SPINACH BAKE

Serves 4   Easy to prepare in a cast-iron skillet, and a good combination of flavors. Cooked chicken can be substituted for the beef if you prefer.

1   pound ground beef
1   onion, chopped
¼   pound mushrooms, sliced
1   (10 oz.) package frozen chopped spinach, thawed
1   can cream of mushroom soup
     garlic powder to taste
     herb seasonings
     seasoned pepper
1   cup grated cheese
     ovenproof skillet—or baking dish

TIP: If you don't have an oven-proof skillet, just transfer mixture to a baking dish and bake as directed. *California burgundy or Zinfandel*

1. In an ovenproof skillet brown beef, onion and mushrooms.
2. Blend in thawed spinach and mushroom soup. Season to taste and mix well.
3. Top with cheese and bake at 350° for 30 minutes or till hot.

ROAST PRIME RIB

Serves 4-6   I only do this for company or a special family dinner, when everyone is "dying" for prime rib. Serve with creamed spinach and Yorkshire pudding. (See index for recipes.)

1   standing rib roast (2-3 ribs) from the small end
     seasoned salt and pepper
     garlic powder
     meat thermometer
     shallow roasting pan

TIP: Yorkshire pudding takes about 30-35 minutes if made in a cast iron skillet. If you only have one oven, place meat in lower part of the oven so the Yorkshire can cook on top rack at the end.
Aged Cabernet, or French Red Burgundy

1. Arrange oven rack. Preheat oven to 350° (see Tip).
2. Sprinkle seasonings all over meat.
3. Place fat side up in pan. (Bones make a natural rack.) Place meat thermometer in the center of the rib eye muscle by inserting from the side.
4. Roast in oven until thermometer reads 130° to 140° (20-25 minutes per pound), unless everyone in your household likes their meat well done.
5. Remove from oven and cover with foil while meat sets up and Yorkshire pudding is being finished (15-20 minutes).
6. Slice in ¾" slices, serving the end cuts to those who prefer well done servings. The center should be medium rare.

ROAST BEEF WITH BROWNED POTATOES AND ONIONS

TIP: I have not listed roasting times because it will depend on the *size* of the meat cut, how *thick* the roast is and how *cold it is* when you put it in the oven.

Merlot, French Rhone

Serves 4-6

This was created when I was in a hurry and it has turned out to be a favorite. I prefer to use a boned rump roast because it is lean and easy to carve. This recipe can be duplicated with a roasting chicken, if desired, but cook the chicken well done.

flat roasting pan with a rack*
1   *boneless lean roast* (3-5 pounds)*
3-4 *potatoes, scrubbed and cut up*
2-3 *onions, cut into chunks*
2-3 *large carrots, cut up (optional)*
     seasoned salt and pepper
½   *cube margarine, melted*
½   *cup dry wine, red or rose*
     meat thermometer

   *See meat tips and roasting principles.

1. Preheat oven to 350⁰.
2. Place the meat on the rack in the pan. Place scrubbed potatoes and the onions below the meat on the bottom of the pan. Season with salt and pepper.
3. Place the meat thermometer in the center of the meat muscle and then baste the meat and vegetables with the margarine and wine, which has been mixed together.
4. Place the pan into the oven and roast at 350⁰—rare to medium. (About 140⁰-150⁰ on meat thermometer.) *If you cook this well done, it will be dry and tough.**
5. Baste the vegetables every 15-20 minutes with the wine mixture, or any drippings that accumulate. *They should get brown and crispy.* They need about 1½ hours.
6. Slice the roast *very thin* and place the meat on a platter and place the vegetables around the meat. Pour drippings on the meat and vegetables, and serve with pride.

PEPPER STEAK

Serves 4

Better known as "Steak Diane." This is my own version done at school to show flaming technique. It's delicious and very popular.

Cabernet or Pinot Noir

1-2 tablespoons whole black peppercorns
1 kitchen towel
1 meat pounder
1 flank steak
½ cube butter
¼ cup brandy, heated
½ cup heavy cream
  large cast iron skillet
  wood board or flat surface
  serving platter

1. Place peppercorns in closed towel and pound them to break open.
2. Lay flank steak on towel. Put half the peppercorns on one side of the meat.
3. Fold towel over meat and pound peppercorns into meat. Turn over and repeat on the other side, so each side has pepper imbedded in it.
4. Melt butter in the skillet on medium high heat and add the peppered steak. Saute on one side for about 5 minutes. Turn and continue to cook until desired degree of doneness. (Make a small cut in flank steak to check redness.)
5. Remove meat from heat. Warm brandy and light with a match, so it flames. *Carefully* pour brandy over meat and stir to keep flame up, so brandy will burn off. *Be very careful since fat will tend to flame up as well.*
6. Remove meat to serving platter.
7. Add cream to skillet and reduce on medium high heat until thickened. Taste for seasoning.
8. Slice flank at an angle and pour reduced cream sauce over meat and serve with pride.

BEEF STROGANOFF

 Merlot, French Rhone

Serves 4

This is a nice variation and a most popular one. Serve over cooked noodles or rice.

1   pound top round steak
1   teaspoon seasoned salt
¼   teaspoon pepper
½   teaspoon leaf basil
1   garlic clove, minced
1-2 tablespoons oil
½   pound sliced mushrooms
2   onions, sliced
⅔   cup beef broth
⅔   cup sherry or Vermouth
1   cup sour cream
1   large deep fry pan
    cooked noodles or rice
    minced parsley

1. Cut meat into thin 2" strips and place in a mixing bowl. Add the salt, pepper, basil, garlic, and a little oil. Mix seasoning into meat by hand. Set aside.

2. In the fry pan, saute the mushrooms and sliced onions in a little oil. Remove and set aside.

3. In the same pan, saute seasoned meat for a few minutes. Add sauteed vegetables, broth and wine. Simmer gently for 45 minutes on low heat. Add more liquid if needed or cover if you wish.

4. Just before serving, when mixture is hot and noodles are ready, add sour cream and heat to serving temperature. *Do not boil or mixture will curdle.*

5. Serve over noodles or rice and garnish with parsley.

VEAL "NICOISE"

Serves 2

When I was on one of my rare "diets," I created this dish and it hit the spot. You could use chicken filet if you wish. Vary the seasonings as you like.

Light red, French rose

¾ *pound of veal round scallops*
¼ *cup finely chopped parsley*
2 *large garlic cloves, minced*
1 *tablespoon Parmesan cheese*
2-3 *tablespoons olive oil*
10 *(to 15) Nicoise style olives*
2-3 *tablespoons Vermouth or wine*
    salt and pepper
½ *lemon*
12" non-stick skillet

1. Gently pound parsley, garlic and cheese into veal pieces.
2. In the large skillet, heat the olive oil on medium high heat. When oil is hot, brown veal on each side for a minute or two.
3. Toss in olives and deglaze with wine. Season with a little salt and pepper.
4. Squeeze a bit of lemon juice over veal and serve with pan juice.

SHISH KABOB'S

Serves 4-6

I prefer to use veal stew or shoulder meat but it works well with beef or lamb. This is a great company dish where you have "guests" who like their meat cooked differently.

TIP: You don't need to do this ahead—it just tastes better if it marinates for awhile before you cook it.
Vigorous Red, Rose

½ *cup olive oil*
¼ *cup lemon juice*
1 *teaspoon salt*
1 *teaspoon leaf marjoram*
1 *teaspoon leaf thyme*
½ *teaspoon pepper*
2 *cloves garlic, minced*
½ *cup chopped green onion*
¼ *cup minced parsley*
2 *pounds boneless meat cut in 1½"-2" cubes*
2 *green peppers in wedges*
1 *onion in wedges*

1. In a large bowl, combine oil, lemon juice, salt, marjoram, thyme, pepper, garlic, chopped onion and parsley. Add meat and stir to coat.
2. Refrigerate several hours or overnight, turning meat occasionally to marinate well.
3. Alternately skewer meat cubes, wedges of green pepper and onion.
4. Broil on high or BBQ over hot coals until brown, turning and brushing often with marinade. Plan on 15-20 minutes, depending on meat temperatures and desired degree of doneness.

PORK CHOPS WITH WINE 'N HERBS

A fruity wine, white or rose that is similar to what you cooked with.

Serves 4

People just love pork this way! Encourage your friends to chew on the bones if they like.

The chops for this recipe must be 1½ to 2" thick. Pork is raised to be much leaner today so you must not over cook it or it will be tough and dry.

4   center cut pork chops, at least 1" thick
1   teaspoon sage leaves, crumbled*
1   teaspoon dried rosemary, crumbled
1   teaspoon minced garlic
¼   teaspoon salt
¼   teaspoon freshly ground black pepper
1   tablespoon butter
1   tablespoon olive oil
1   cup white or rose wine
1   tablespoon finely chopped fresh parsley
     10-12" covered saute pan
If you can't find leaf sage & rosemary you may substitute 1-2 teaspoons of mixed herbs, but try to use sage and rosemary as it gives the recipe a special flavor.

1. Trim almost all the fat off the chops.
2. Crush the sage, rosemary, garlic, salt, and pepper together and press a little of this mixture firmly into both sides of each pork chop.
3. In the skillet melt the butter with the olive oil over moderate heat. When the foam subsides, place the chops in the hot fat and brown them well on each side.
4. When the chops are brown pour off any excess fat. Add ¾ cup of wine to the chops and bring to a boil. Reduce heat to an active simmer and cook *covered* for 10 to 15 minutes, or until they just lose their pinkness. Turn over in the juices every so often.
5. Remove cooked chops to a plate and keep warm. Add remainder of wine to skillet and boil mixture briskly over high heat, stirring in any browned bits that cling to the pan.
6. Continue to boil until you have reduced the mixture to a syrupy glaze. Pour a little glaze on each one of the chops. Garnish with parsley and serve.

Boned loin of Pork is a great cut of meat that people really enjoy.
    Just oven roast or BBQ on a slow fire till meat is 150° - 160°
                    (medium well)
Season to taste - Slice ½" thick for an easy - Delicious treat.

BARBEQUED SPARERIBS

I have included not only two sauce recipes but two methods of cooking. One sauce is from "scratch" and the other uses prepared sauces. Both are great and can be used with a variety of meat or chicken. Try it on a pork roast.

Homemade Sauce

½   cup honey
¼   cup crushed pineapple
½   cup pineapple juice
½   cup catsup
1   teaspoon salt
¼   cup sherry wine
⅓   cup light molasses or Karo syrup
½   cup hot barbeque sauce
    rack of ribs
    basting brush
    BBQ fire (covered kettle type is preferred for smoke flavor and control)

Easy Sauce

1   bottle of good hot spicy BBQ sauce (Chris & Pitts)
½   bottle of Lawry's Sweet and Sour
½   cup rose wine

Directions for Both Recipes

1. Mix sauce ingredients together and set aside.
2. Place ribs over a *slow, indirect fire* if possible and begin cooking.*
3. After 30-40 minutes of cooking, coat the ribs with sauce and continue cooking—basting regularly—making certain the ribs do not flame or catch fire.
4. Cook ribs until medium-well and nice and brown—about 2 hours, depending on the heat source and the method of cooking.

*A hotter direct fire will cook them faster but might burn them.

Oven Method   This works well and is very easy since you don't have to worry about the ribs burning.

1. Lay ribs on a foil covered flat broiler pan and brush liberally with sauce. Roast 350°-400° until cooked and brown—about 1½ to 2 hours.
2. Baste regularly with the sauce during cooking and turn ribs over if the underside is not browning properly.

TIP: Although some people recommend boiling ribs ahead of time to speed cooking and remove fat, you also lose the valuable B vitamin thiamin in the water.

Chenin blanc, rose or young red

BAKED HAM

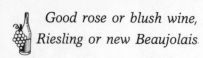

Good rose or blush wine,
Riesling or new Beaujolais

Ham has always been popular at our house. It's traditional for my family to serve it at Easter time and of course when we are in the mood for it. Ham has real sentimental value for me—my dad, being a Southerner, loved a good ham or a *Virginia* ham when we could get it.

Also, the day I introduced my husband to my parents, in 1968, it was Easter Sunday and I fixed ham.

1   *quality rump shank (bone in, if possible)**
1   *cup rose or similar wine*
2   *teaspoons prepared mustard*
¼   *cup brown sugar*
1/8 *teaspoon ground cloves*
    cloves for decorating (optional)
    pastry brush
    parsley sprigs
    roasting pan

*Canned ham can be substituted but it is not quite as good

1. Score ham, if desired, and place in roasting pan. (Foil line, if you do not want to use drippings.)

2. In a small bowl, mix wine, mustard, sugar and ground cloves. Brush all over ham and then dot with whole cloves, if desired.

3. Roast at 350° degrees for a few hours or until ham is hot throughout (140°) and brown. Baste and continue to brush with sauce as the ham bakes.

4. Remove from oven and let sit for about 15 minutes covered with foil. Thinly slice and arrange on a platter garnished with parsley.

POULTRY

POULTRY TIPS

1. Poultry is selected according to the kind–e.g. broiler, fryer or roaster, and by the weight.
2. Since poultry is quite perishable, it should be used within a day or two, or frozen for future use.
3. Fresh poultry products carry bacteria, so proper *storage, preparation, washing* and *cooking techniques* are *extremely* important.
4. Modern poultry is raised to be very tender so it only needs to be cooked until done. (Flesh cooked and juices run clear). If you overcook most poultry it will produce a dry and toughened product.

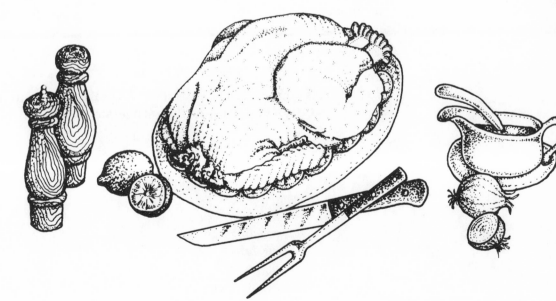

ROAST TURKEY AND DRESSING

TIP: Plan to have the turkey done at least one hour or so before serving time, so you can make the gravy and use the oven for other things if needed.

Young Zinfandel, Beaujolais, Rose

19-25 pound turkey

For years, my mother and I have been stuffing turkeys at Thanksgiving and Christmas. We really made it up over the years with lots of advice from other family members. *Never* stuff the bird until right before you cook it.

Stuffing

This mixture is great for stuffing chicken, fish, pork chops or even vegetables.

2½	cubes margarine or butter
1	large onion, chopped
1	large bunch of green onions, chopped (usually from my mom's garden)
5	celery stalks, chopped
1½	pounds mushrooms, sliced
½	cup chopped parsley
1	box seasoned stuffing mix (2 bags)
	poultry seasonings
	dry Vermouth or rose wine or broth
	pepper
	large skillet
	large bowl

I use more onion & parsley but all the ingredients should be adjusted depending on bird size & personal preferences.

1. In a large skillet, melt margarine or butter, and add onions, celery, mushrooms and parsley. Saute for about 5 minutes.

2. Place desired amount of stuffing mix in the bowl. Blend in sauteed veggies and season to taste with poultry seasoning and pepper. Add some wine or broth if you need some moisture. Remember, dressing will get *more* moist in the bird, so adjust according to your taste.

3. Stuff bird immediately and begin to roast. *Put extra stuffing in a casserole and bake in the oven the last 45 minutes while gravy is being made.*

Turkey Portion

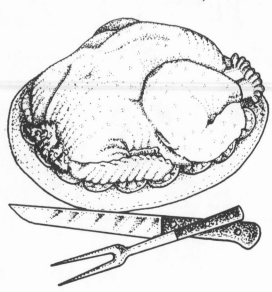

If you buy a frozen bird, it will take a minimum of 2-3 days to defrost in the refrigerator.

1	19-25 pound turkey
½	cup melted margarine
½	cup dry Vermouth or rose wine
	metal skewers
	metal roasting rack
	flat roasting pan
	basting brush
	carving board
	good slicing knife

1. Remove neck and giblets and wash them. Place in a saucepan and cover with water and some vegetable trimmings.*

2. Simmer giblets for 1 or 2 hours. Save broth for gravy.* (Feed neck and giblets to anyone who wants them.)

3. As giblets begin to cook, put turkey in the sink and wash with cold water, so water runs in and out of bird.

4. Dry bird and keep chilled, unless you are ready with the stuffing.*

5. Stuff the bird lightly under the neck skin and skewer closed. Turn over and *lightly* put the stuffing into the body cavity so it is full but not packed. (If you pack it too tightly it can't heat properly by the time the turkey is done.)

6. Preheat oven to 325⁰ and arrange rack in proper oven position.

7. Tie legs together or secure area with skin piece. Carefully lift bird on-to prepared roasting rack in the roasting pan.

8. Brush turkey with mixed margarine and wine. Arrange meat thermometer (if you have one) in thickest part of thigh muscle. Many birds have pop thermometers in the breast that need to be set.

9. Place in preheated oven and begin roasting, basting with the wine and butter mixture every half hour or so. Cook until recommended doneness. (See Tip.) Cut legs apart halfway through cooking time.

10. When turkey is done, remove from oven and remove turkey carefully from rack (have help, please) onto carving board. Cover entire bird with foil to keep warm.

*These first steps may be done the night before if you wish.

TIMING: Our turkeys always get done sooner than the recommended times. As a guide figure *3-4 hours at 325°*, adjusting for individual birds, temperature of the uncooked bird and size of your oven.

Temperature in the thigh should register 175⁰ or in the breast 160⁰, or until the meat is *not* pink but still juicy. The leg should begin to move freely in the joint— but if it starts to fall off, it is too done. Sorry!

Gravy

	jar for slurry
1	cup water
½	cup flour
	reserved broth from giblets
	turkey drippings
	salt and pepper
	large saucepan
	wire whip

1. In the jar, shake up flour and water together to make a smooth slurry.

2. Pour and scrape all the drippings from the roasting pan into the saucepan.

3. Remove about one half the *grease* from the drippings and discard.

4. Shake slurry again and add mixture to drippings. Using a wire whip, thoroughly mix slurry and drippings together. Add some broth and continue to stir.

5. On medium-high heat, bring gravy to a boil, stirring constantly. Add more broth to thin, if necessary. Continue to simmer and season to taste. About 15 minutes before serving, *when everything is ready*, remove stuffing to serving dish. Slice turkey—and get ready for a feast . . . forget about the *dishes*.

Be sure and chill leftover turkey as soon as possible. Keep only 4-5 days in the refrigerator. It's almost easier to break up the carcass and freeze the bones or make soup in a day or two & freeze

OVER-FRIED CHICKEN

This is still Bob's favorite — but always with hot biscuits

Serves 3-4

This recipe was a result of my helping with chicken for 500 persons at a church supper. I created this recipe from that experience and it is my husband's favorite dish. It is so easy that every piece of chicken is good this way—even backs and necks. It should be served with good biscuits.

1   3-4 pound broiler-fryer, cut up
½   cup Bisquick or flour
1   teaspoon seasoned salt
1/8 teaspoon seasoned pepper
       garlic powder
1   tablespoon Parmesan cheese
½   teaspoon dried herbs (optional)
1   cube margarine, melted
       pastry brush
       large, flat baking dish or flat roasting pan

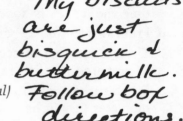

My biscuits are just bisquick & buttermilk. Follow box directions.

1. Preheat oven to 500⁰.
2. Wash chicken and dry. Line flat pan with foil for easier cleaning.*
3. In a bowl or bag, mix Bisquick and dry seasonings. Dredge chicken pieces in flour mixture and lay skin side up in the flat baking pan. Try to keep pieces from touching, if possible.
4. Brush melted margarine liberally on each piece of chicken. Place chicken in a preheated 500⁰ oven preferably in the top portion of the oven.
5. Continue to bake at 500⁰ until the chicken begins to brown, about 15-20 minutes. Lower the oven to 375⁰ to 400⁰ and finish cooking until the chicken is brown and crispy (about 1 hour). Serve warm or cold.

*If you want to make chicken gravy from drippings, don't line pan with foil. Use a flat metal pan or the bottom of a broiler pan so you can transfer it from the oven to the surface for the gravy preparation.

Microwave Instructions

Faster but not as brown and crispy.

1. Use a glass baking dish and do not line with foil.
2. Prepare chicken the same way only cook on high power for 15 to 25 minutes. The time will vary depending on how cold the chicken is and how fast your microwave cooks, since different models vary.
3. Brown chicken under a broiler for a few minutes if necessary.

Sandi & Angie Zupan — friends from Oregon couldn't believe that this chicken w/gravy & biscuits is standard fare on the Karlin dinner table. When Sandi asked me for the recipe — she said "I know - its in the Book"!

CHICKEN CHEZ KARLIN

Serves 4

This was created by accident as it is one of those "little-bit-of-this-and-that" recipes. It's easy and flexible since you can add or subtract, depending on your taste. Serve this mixture on top of hot pasta.

TIP: This dish can be prepared ahead of time to the end of step 3, and finished 15 minutes before dinner is served.

Dry rose, Zinfandel, Red Rhone

large skillet with lid
2 *tablespoons olive oil*
4 *Italian sausages*
4-6 *chicken pieces*
1 *large onion, finely sliced*
1 *green pepper, sliced*
4 *green onions, chopped*
½ *pound mushrooms, sliced*
2 *large garlic cloves, minced*
1-2 *teaspoons Italian herbs*
2 *tablespoons fresh parsley, chopped*
seasoned salt and pepper
1 *cup white or rose wine*
1 *(8 oz.) can stewed tomatoes*
1 *(10 oz.) pkg. frozen french style green beans, thawed**
¾ *pound spaghetti*
½ *cup freshly grated Parmesan cheese*
chopped parsley for garnish

Fresh green beans may be substituted but they will need longer cooking time.

1. In the skillet, brown sausages until they are just done—10-12 minutes. Poke as they cook so some fat will be released. Set sausages aside.

2. In the same skillet, brown the chicken pieces in oil if needed. Set well-browned chicken aside and add the onions, green pepper, green onions, mushrooms and garlic to the skillet. Saute on high for a few minutes.

3. Put the chicken back with the vegetables and season with the herbs, salt and pepper. Add the wine and the tomatoes and cover. Simmer the whole mixture for about 10-15 minutes or until the chicken just loses its pinkness. (See tip.)

4. At this point, you can begin to prepare the spaghetti.

5. About 10-15 minutes before you are ready to eat, remove the lid and add the sausage and thawed green beans. Set the lid slightly ajar, then boil the whole mixture until the sausage and beans are hot and the sauce has cooked down a little. *Be sure you watch it and don't overcook the chicken or lose your color in the green beans.*

6. Serve over hot pasta. Give each person a piece of chicken and sausage and then lots of the vegetables with the sauce.

7. Garnish with some cheese and fresh parsley.

POULET SAUTE AU FROMAGE

Beaujolais, young Cabernet, Pinot Noir

Serves 4

(Chicken with cheese) This dish was created accidentally and is really a winner. It's great for large parties because you can do it ahead.

4-6 *chicken breasts, boned and skinned*
4 *slices of bacon, cut in half*
1 *bunch green onions, chopped*
¾ *cup white wine*
pepper
½ *cup Swiss cheese, grated*
2 *tablespoons parsley, chopped*
large skillet with lid

1. Wash and dry chicken breasts and set aside.
2. In the skillet, fry bacon until fat is released and then add onions and continue frying for a few minutes.
3. Add chicken breasts and brown lightly on each side.
4. Add ½ cup of wine, some pepper and cover. Simmer chicken on low until just cooked, about 5 minutes. (Boned breasts cook rapidly, especially when they have already been browned.)
5. Remove cover and sprinkle each breast with some cheese and parsley. Replace cover and cook for a few minutes more.
6. When ready to serve, remove chicken to serving plates. Add remaining wine to deglaze skillet. Scrape up any brown bits and then boil sauce to thicken. Pour a little reduced sauce on chicken and serve. (Bacon may be served to those who want it.)

CHICKEN ROQUEFORT

Zinfandel, Cabernet Sauvignon, Medium Dry White

Serves 4

Bob and I finally made it to the caves of Roquefort this summer and returned with a big wheel of cheese. This recipe is a nice change of "pace."

4-6 *chicken breasts*
½ *cube butter*
2-3 *tablespoons Roquefort or bleu cheese*
1 *garlic clove, minced*
broiler pan

1. Wash and dry chicken breasts. Slash skins of breasts in a few places.
2. In a small bowl, cream butter, cheese and garlic together. Spread some mixed butter on both sides of chicken so that a little is under the skin.
3. Place breasts skin side *down* on broiler pan and broil 4"-5" from heat source until brown (10-12 minutes). Turn over and continue broiling until chicken is cooked and brown. Baste if you can with juices that run off chicken, or with any extra butter you may have. Serve hot . . . mmmmmm!

CHICKEN WITH WINE 'N HERBS

Serves 6   So easy, but a real company dish because people   *White or Rose*
think it's fancy. Delicious with rice pilaf.

2   tablespoons butter or oil
6   chicken breasts
    seasoned salt and pepper
½   teaspoon crushed dried herbs
    (thyme, basil or marjoram)
2   tablespoons fresh parsley
½   pound mushrooms, sliced
1   bunch green onions, chopped
¾   cup white or rose wine
    10'' skillet with lid

Skinned chicken pieces will work fine if you prefer

1. In the skillet, quickly brown the chicken in the butter. Season with salt, pepper and herbs.
2. Add the sliced mushrooms and onion. Continue to saute the chicken for a few minutes. Add the wine to the skillet and cover.
3. Simmer mixture for about 15 to 20 minutes until the chicken is done and the sauce has cooked down a little.* (Add more wine or liquid if necessary.) Taste for seasoning.
4. Remove chicken to serving plates and reduce sauce to thicken somewhat.
5. Serve with rice on the side and spoon the sauce over the chicken and rice, if desired.

*A nice variation would be to add some artichoke hearts and chopped tomato to the simmering chicken near the end.

TANDOORI CHICKEN

White or Rose   Serves 4

My friend Denise in San Francisco shared this recipe with me as well as the spice mix which we purchased on our infamous shopping trips to Cost Plus. Broil or BBQ chicken for this "Indian" dish.

1   *whole chicken—cut up*
1   *cup of plain, unflavored yogurt*
1-2 *teaspoons tandoori spice mix**
1-2 *teaspoons of oil*
    salt and pepper

*Available in specialty food stores.

1. Wash and dry chicken pieces. Slash skin on each piece in several places.
2. In a large bowl, mix up yogurt, spice, oil, salt and pepper to taste.
3. Place chicken pieces in yogurt mix and coat completely with marinade (do ahead if possible).
4. Broil or BBQ on low "fire" for about 20-25 minutes, turning often to brush with yogurt marinade. Watch that chicken doesn't stick to grill.
5. Cook till chicken is not pink and it is brown and crispy on the outside.

CURRIED CHICKEN 'N RICE

Fruity Blush wine, Riesling   Serves 4
or Gewurtztraminer

This is easy and the combinations of flavors is pleasing. This can be made ahead and reheated.

1   *chicken, cut up*
¼   *cup butter or oil*
1   *large green pepper, chopped*
2   *garlic cloves, minced*
1   *large onion, chopped*
1   *cup uncooked rice*
1   *(1 pound) can tomatoes*
1-2 *teaspoons curry powder*
1   *teaspoon thyme*
1   *tablespoon cilantro or Italian parsley*
     seasoned salt and pepper to taste
1½   *cups dry white wine*
     large skillet with lid

1. Brown chicken in butter. Remove chicken and set aside.
2. Add green pepper, garlic, onion and rice to the same pan and stir until lightly browned.
3. Stir in tomatoes, seasonings, and wine. Add browned chicken to mixture. Cover and cook on a low simmer until chicken and rice are done, adding more liquid if necessary (approximately 30 minutes).
4. Taste for seasoning and serve.

CHICKEN KIEV

12 servings

This takes a little time and planning but it is well worth the effort if people appreciate a good Kiev.

Safety Tip: Deep frying must be done with caution. Make sure you cook in a safe place—and avoid any water near the hot oil.
Pinot Noir, Chardonnay

Herb Butter

1   cup butter (2 cubes) softened
2   tablespoons chopped parsley
1½ teaspoons dried tarragon
1   garlic clove
½   teaspoon seasoned salt
1/8 teaspoon pepper

Chicken

6   boned and skinned whole chicken breasts
¾   cup flour
3   eggs, well beaten
1½ cups dry bread crumbs
     oil for frying
     pan for 3" deep frying
     toothpicks or skewers
     waxed paper or plastic wrap

1. In a small bowl, mix butter and seasonings for herb butter. On a piece of foil, shape the butter into a 6" square. Freeze until firm.
2. While butter is freezing, wash and dry chicken. Cut each breast in half.
3. To flatten chicken, place each half, smooth side down, on a sheet of waxed paper. Cover with more waxed paper. Pound chicken to about ¼" thickness, being careful not to tear the meat. Repeat on all the breasts.
4. Cut frozen butter in 12 even pieces. Place one piece of herb butter in the center of each piece of chicken. Bring long sides of chicken over butter and then fold ends in, making sure that butter is covered completely and you have a fairly tight package. Fasten chicken firmly with small skewers or toothpicks.
5. Dredge each chicken piece in flour, then dip into beaten egg and roll in bread crumbs. Refrigerate chicken pieces till well chilled—about one hour.
6. In a deep pan, electrically controlled, if possible, heat 3-inch deep oil to 375⁰ or medium-high heat.
7. Only when oil is hot enough add 2 or 3 chicken pieces at a time.
8. Fry pieces, turning with tongs until evenly browned—about 5-7 minutes. Drain and then keep in a warm oven until all chicken is finished. Serve as soon as possible since the herb butter will be melted and might tend to run out.

GENERAL BAKING TIPS

1. Use a preheated oven to ensure more even and accurately timed baking.
2. The oven rack and positioning of food will determine browning and rate of cooking. Always allow air circulation around each item to ensure even baking. Place most food in the center portion of the oven to prevent uneven browning or burning.
3. *Never* line oven racks with foil or try to bake with too many pans in the oven at one time, e.g., cookie sheets – since that will destroy even heat patterns so necessary to even browning.
4. Choose your pan material wisely – glass versus metal – since they reflect heat differently and determine rate of cooking and amount of browning.
5. It is essential that the recommended pan size is used since it will determine timing and success of the recipe.
6. *Plan ahead* when it comes to mixing bowl size and for multiple jobs. Always prepare pans for baking before you begin a recipe.
7. Do not substitute ingredients unless the recipe indicates it is OK. Shortening will give very different results than butter.
8. Sifting and proper measuring is absolutely essential for success. One extra tablespoon of flour could ruin a cake recipe. *Do not* use liquid measures to measure flour or sugar.
9. Proper techniques, such as beating, creaming, kneading, and order of procedures, will help ensure success.
10. Never open oven doors to check sensitive baked items, or remove from oven until food tests done.

Measuring Tips

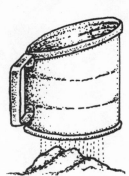 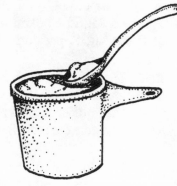 

Sift before measuring   **Spoon lightly into cup. Don't pack.**   **Level off.**

BREADS

GENERAL BREAD TIPS

YEAST BREADS

1. All purpose white flour works fine for yeast breads although unbleached all purpose and specially blended bread flour gives better gluten structure. Whole wheat flour will give heavier, lower gluten textured loaves.
2. Sifting flour before measuring gives *certainty* in the amount you are working with.
3. Proper liquid temperature (115°) will insure proper yeast fermentation. Too hot will kill the yeast and a too cold temperature will slow down or stop the process.
4. Kneading or vigorous mixing is essential to yeast breads to develop gluten for bread structure.
5. Proofing to double in bulk–usually twice in a recipe–is essential for proper flavor, texture and yeast fermentation.
6. Yeast breads may be frozen in the second proof stage or after baking.

QUICK BREADS

1. Proper pan preparation–grease, flour, and lining the bottom ensure successful loaf bread removal.
2. Proper measuring is essential to quick breads.
3. Over mixing will result in tough or dry bread products.
4. It is normal for loaf breads to crack in the middle of the top.
5. Test loaf breads (banana, etc.) by using the cake test for doneness. (see cake tips)
6. Times for doneness will vary according to pan size and temperature of ingredients. Most quick breads take longer to bake than the recipes indicate.

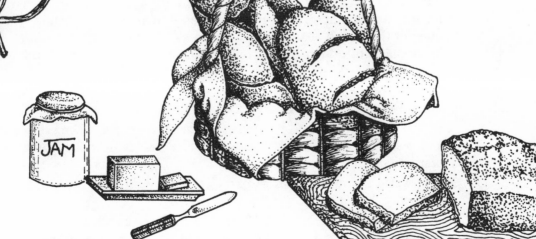

YEAST

Yeast bread takes time & experience to perfect. You need to develop a "hand" for bread since kneading takes practice and flour amounts vary according to many factors.

WHITE BREAD

1 loaf

TIP: A thermometer is foolproof but if you want to "chance" it, 115° feels like *warm* not hot bath water while 100° feels lukewarm.

A warm place 80° – 100° really is needed for proofing the dough although the dough will "grow" at room temp or even in the refrigerator. It just takes longer.

I found this recipe in an old cook book 20 years ago and my students have used this one loaf recipe to learn yeast bread technique for 19 years. (I must have made this loaf 500 times.)

3   cups sifted flour*
½   cup milk, scalded
1   rounded tablespoon butter or margarine
½   teaspoon salt
1   tablespoon sugar
1   package dry yeast
½   cup 115° water (very warm)*
    extra flour
    melted butter
    8½ X 4½ X 2½" glass bread pan*

*See bread tips.

1. Sift and measure flour and set aside.
2. In a small saucepan, scald milk until little bubbles form on the edge of pan. Remove from heat and add butter, salt and sugar. Cool to 100° (use thermometer or your clean finger).
3. When milk is just the correct temperature (100-105°), pour yeast into a large mixing bowl. Add 115° water and dissolve yeast in water. Add milk mixture.
4. Add about 1½ cups flour into warm milk mixture. Beat vigorously.
5. Continue to add some of the remaining flour until dough can be handled for kneading. (Do not add all the flour at once, since you will continue to add while you knead.)
6. Place sticky dough on a floured surface and begin kneading. Knead for 5-8 minutes, adding flour only when dough sticks to hands (you may let the dough rest for a few minutes, if you want); continue kneading until dough is smooth and elastic. (Total time 15-20 minutes.)
7. Place smooth dough into well greased bowl and cover bowl with plastic wrap. Place in a warm (100° oven) place until it doubles in bulk (1½ hours) and a fingerprint impression remains.
8. Punch dough down and compact it to get the air out. Shape into a loaf and place in well-greased glass loaf pan. Brush with melted butter or margarine.
9. In a warm place, let proof in pan to at least double in bulk. (30-45 minutes.)
10. Preheat oven to 400° about 10 minutes before bread is ready. (If bread is in the oven, just place on top of the range during preheat time.)

11. Bake at 400⁰ for about 25 minutes, or until loaf thumps hollow and is very brown.
12. Remove from pan to cooling rack and brush loaf with butter. Cover with towel for 5 minutes to soften crust.
13. Slice with serrated knife carefully from the side to avoid tearing loaf. Enjoy with butter and jam!

WHOLE WHEAT SOUR DOUGH BREAD

2 loaves

My Uncle Freeman in Virginia has had great success with this bread.

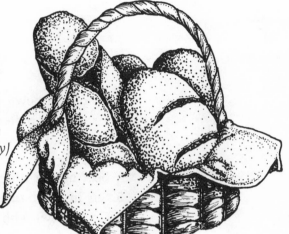

1	cup milk
2	packages yeast
1	cup warm water (115°)
3	cups unsifted whole wheat flour regular or stone ground
¼	cup light molasses
1	tablespoon salt
3	tablespoons soft butter or margarine
3	cups all-purpose flour (approximately) melted butter
2	loaf pans, greased

Sour Dough

1. Scald milk and let cool to lukewarm.
2. In a large bowl, stir yeast into warm water (115⁰) until dissolved.
3. Add lukewarm milk and whole wheat flour; stir to combine. Cover bowl tightly with plastic wrap. Let stand at room temperature for 2 days. Dough will be bubbly and smell like fermenting apple cider.

After 2 Days

1. Stir in molasses, salt and butter. Mix in 2 cups of the all-purpose flour.
2. Turn dough onto board with about 1 cup of the remaining flour and knead until smooth and elastic (about 10 minutes), adding flour as needed until dough is no longer sticky.
3. Place dough in a large greased bowl. Grease top of dough and cover bowl with plastic wrap. Let rise in a warm place until doubled in bulk (approximately 45 minutes).
4. Punch dough down and divide in half. Shape each half into a loaf and place into greased 8½ X 4½" loaf pans.
5. Coat loaves with butter. Cover and let rise in a warm place until almost doubled in size (about 45 minutes).
6. About 10 minutes before loaves are ready to bake, preheat oven to 375⁰.
7. Bake for 35 minutes or until nicely browned on top. Remove from pans and cool on racks.

CHEESE HERB CASSEROLE BREAD

6 servings   Make in small casseroles, if you can.

1   *package dry yeast*
¼   *cup warm water (115°)*
¾   *cup milk*
1   *tablespoon butter*
1   *tablespoon minced onion*
½   *teaspoon preferred herb (dill, parsley)*
2   *tablespoons sugar*
1   *teaspoon salt*
1   *egg*
1¼   *cups sifted flour*
1¼   *cups whole wheat flour*
1½   *cups grated cheddar cheese*
⅓   *cup Parmesan cheese*
6   *small (1 cup) casseroles*

1. In a large bowl, sprinkle yeast over warm water (115°).
2. Heat milk, butter, onion, herbs, sugar and salt to 110°.
3. When milk mixture is lukewarm (100°), pour into yeast and stir well.
4. Add egg and half the flour and beat well. Add remaining flour and beat until a sticky dough forms.
5. Stir in 1 cup of cheddar and all the Parmesan cheese.
6. Cover bowl with plastic wrap and let rise until double in bulk (1-1½ hours).
7. Stir dough down and divide among well greased, small 1-2 cups casseroles or custard cups. Sprinkle with remaining cheese.
8. Let rise for 20-30 minutes in a warm place until almost double in bulk.
9. Preheat oven to 350°, 10 minutes before baking time.
10. Bake for 25-30 minutes until bread is brown and thoroughly baked.
11. Remove from dishes and cool.

BASIC ROLL DOUGH

*TIP: Substitute 1 cup of whole wheat flour for 1 cup of the white flour.

2-3 dozen   May be used for a sweet bread or any type of dinner rolls.

4   *cups sifted flour* (See Tip)*
1   *package dry yeast*
1¼   *cups milk*
¼   *cup sugar*
¼   *cup shortening or margarine*
1   *teaspoon salt*
1   *egg*

     *See bread tips.

1. In a mixing bowl, combine 1½ cups of the flour and the yeast.
2. In a saucepan, heat milk, sugar, shortening and salt until warm (115⁰-120⁰) and the shortening begins to melt.
3. Blend into dry mixture. Add the egg and beat vigorously for a few minutes. Stir in remaining flour or enough to make a *soft dough that you can handle.*
4. Knead a minute or so to make sure dough is not too sticky and is well mixed.
5. Place dough in a large greased bowl. Cover with plastic wrap. Let rise until double in bulk in a warm place (80⁰-100⁰).
6. Punch down and shape into rolls, as desired. Place on greased sheets or pans and let rise till double in bulk.
7. Bake in a preheated 400⁰ oven for 10 to 12 minutes.

MOTHER'S CINNAMON ROLLS

15-20 rolls
We had these delicious yeast rolls at home when I was growing up. I adapted them for school and this is one of my best sellers.

1 basic roll dough recipe,
   or 1 box yeast dough mix
1 cube margarine
¾ of (1 lb.) box of light brown sugar
2 teaspoons cinnamon
   nuts and raisins (optional)
¼ cup melted margarine
   pastry brush
   greased 9 X 13" glass baking pan
   aluminum foil

1. Make basic roll dough and let rise until double in bulk. (See recipe.)
2. Punch dough down. On a floured surface, pat dough to approximately a 17 X 10" rectangle.
3. In a saucepan, melt margarine and stir in brown sugar.
4. Spread sugar mixture evenly over entire surface of yeast dough. Sprinkle with cinnamon (and nuts and raisins, if desired.)
5. Roll from 17" end, jelly roll fashion. Cut 1½ inch slices. Place cut side down so slices barely touch. Brush with melted margarine and let rise in a warm place until doubled in bulk.
6. About 10 minutes before rolls are ready to bake, preheat oven to 425⁰. Bake for 15-20 minutes, or until brown and baked through.
7. Remove from oven and carefully *flip entire pan* of rolls onto aluminum foil. (Rolls and syrup will be very hot, so use extreme caution.)
8. Let cool, until you won't burn your mouth, and then pull apart and enjoy.

"ICE BOX" ROLLS

3 dozen   The recipe was given to me by an old friend. You can refrigerate these rolls up to three days.

¾ cup milk
6   tablespoons margarine or butter
6   tablespoons sugar
1½ teaspoons salt
1   package dry yeast
¼   cup warm water (115°)
1   egg
3½ cups sifted flour
    melted butter or margarine
    cookie sheet

1. In a saucepan, scald the milk. Add the butter, sugar and salt and stir until dissolved. Cool until warm (about 100°).
2. In a mixing bowl, dissolve the yeast in the warm water (115°). Beat in the egg. Stir the warm milk mixture into the yeast mixture.
3. Beat in ½ the flour. Beat dough for 2 minutes. Add the rest of the flour and beat until the dough blisters.
4. Place in a large greased bowl. Cover with plastic wrap and refrigerate. (Best if chilled for 24 hours.)
5. About *four hours* before baking, roll out and shape into small rolls or as desired. Butter and let rise in warm place.
6. Bake at 425° for 5-8 minutes. WATCH carefully as they will brown very rapidly.

GARLIC BREAD A LA KARLIN

Serves 6-8   Easy to do—vary amounts accordingly.

½ small loaf of sour dough bread,
    or small flute sliced in half lengthwise
1   cube butter, softened
¼   cup mayonnaise
¼   cup Parmesan cheese
    garlic puree or garlic powder to taste
    paprika
    cookie sheet

1. Prepare bread in desired shape—sliced, or a whole long loaf sliced in half, lengthwise.
2. Beat together butter, mayonnaise, cheese and garlic. Spread evenly on bread slices.
3. Sprinkle with paprika and broil until lightly brown and bubbly. *Watch so it does not burn.* Serve hot.

I'm amazed at how many people refrigerate bread when it stales faster in the frig than at room temp. Bread should be frozen for best storage.

QUICK

MOTHER'S NUT BREAD

1 loaf — As a kid, Mother would send this to school in my lunch pail, with butter between the slices. It's great toasted, too.

4 cups sifted flour
¾ cup sugar
1 teaspoon salt
2 teaspoons baking powder
1 egg, beaten
1½ cups milk
1 cup chopped walnuts
loaf pan

1. Preheat oven to 350⁰. Grease and flour one loaf pan.
2. In a bowl, sift together the flour, sugar, salt and baking powder.
3. Mix the egg and milk together and stir into the flour mixture until blended. Fold in nuts.
4. Pour into prepared pan and let it sit 30 minutes to rise. Bake at 350⁰ for 45 minutes.
5. Cool and wrap well to keep from drying out. This stores well in the refrigerator.

OLIVE CHEESE BREAD

1 loaf — A nice change that's not sweet. It's a good snack food, too.

3 cups biscuit mix
2 tablespoons sugar
1 cup buttermilk
1 egg
1 cup grated Swiss cheese
1 cup pimiento stuffed olives, drained and sliced in half
prepared loaf pan

1. Preheat oven to 350⁰. Grease and flour one loaf pan.
2. In a mixing bowl, stir biscuit mix and sugar.
3. Beat buttermilk and egg together and then blend into dry mixture. Beat one minute until well blended. (Mixture will be thick.)
4. Gently stir in cheese and olives until evenly distributed. Spoon into prepared loaf pan and bake at 350⁰ for about 55-60 minutes until it tests done in the center, with a toothpick. (Bread will usually show a crack along the top of the loaf.)
5. Cool five minutes before carefully removing from the pan. Serve warm or rewarm.

ZUCCHINI BREAD

TIP: Add 1 ripe mashed banana with zucchini if you like.

2 loaves

Moist like a cake, freezes for months.

3   eggs
2   cups sugar
1   cup oil
1   tablespoon vanilla
2   cups grated zucchini (See Tip)
2   cups sifted flour
2   teaspoons cinnamon
2   teaspoons baking soda
¼   teaspoon baking powder
1   teaspoon salt
1   cup chopped walnuts (optional)
     electric mixer
2   prepared loaf pans

1. Preheat oven to 350⁰. Grease and flour pans and line pan bottoms with waxed paper.
2. In a large bowl, beat eggs until frothy. Beat in sugar, oil and vanilla until thick.
3. Stir in zucchini and *sifted* dry ingredients. Fold in nuts. Pour mixture into 2 *prepared* loaf pans.
4. Bake at 350⁰ for 1 hour or until bread tests done—when a toothpick pulls clean from the center.
5. Allow bread to cool in pans for 15 minutes, then remove carefully from pans and cool completely on a cooling rack.

PUMPKIN BREAD

2-3 loaves

A must in your quick bread library. Delicious spread with whipped cream and cinnamon. This bread freezes beautifully.

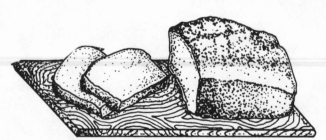

3   cups sugar
1   cup solid shortening or oil
4   eggs
1   teaspoon vanilla
3½   cups sifted flour
1   teaspoon nutmeg
1½   teaspoons cinnamon
2   teaspoons salt
2   teaspoons baking soda
⅔   cup water
2   cups pumpkin
1   cup chopped nuts (optional)
       electric mixer
2-3 loaf pans

1. Preheat oven to 350⁰. Grease, flour and line bottoms of 2-3 bread pans.
2. In a *very* large mixing bowl, cream sugar and shortening until fluffy. Beat in eggs, one at a time, and then the vanilla.
3. Sift flour with nutmeg, cinnamon, salt and soda. Add dry ingredients alternately with water to egg mixture, beating after each addition, until smooth and fluffy.
4. Beat in pumpkin until blended. Add nuts, if desired.
5. Pour into prepared pans and bake until bread tests done like a cake. (One hour or more for large loaves.) Loaves usually will split on the top.*)

*See baking tips.

BANANA-APRICOT BRAN BREAD

1 loaf   A nutritious, tasty combination.

> 2   cups sifted flour
> 2   tablespoons bran
> 2   tablespoons wheat germ
> 1   teaspoon baking powder
> ¾   teaspoon baking soda
> ½   teaspoon salt
> 1   cup sugar
> ½   cup chopped canned apricots
> ¾   cup mashed banana
> ½   cup buttermilk or sour milk*
> 1   egg
> ¼   cup melted butter (½ cube)
> 1   loaf pan
>
> *Sour milk by adding a teaspoon of lemon juice to ½ cup milk.

1. Preheat oven to 350⁰. Grease, flour and line pan.
2. In a bowl, mix flour, bran, wheat germ, baking powder, baking soda, salt and sugar.
3. Mix together the remaining ingredients and stir into dry mixture until just blended.
4. Pour mixture into prepared pan. Bake at 350⁰ until it tests done, approximately 1 hour and 15 minutes.

CHOCOLATE DATE NUT BREAD

1 loaf   An interesting combination that is really delicious.

If you can't locate liquid chocolate use 2 squares of block chocolate and add some oil to it to make it liquid.

1	cup boiling water
1	cup chopped dates
½	cup butter (1 cube)
1	cup sugar
1	egg
1	teaspoon vanilla
2	envelopes liquid* unsweetened chocolate
2	cups sifted flour
½	teaspoon salt
1	teaspoon baking soda
½	cup chopped pecans
	prepared loaf pan

*Liquid chocolate must be used since bread dough is very thick.

1. Preheat oven to 350º. Grease and flour one loaf pan.
2. Pour boiling water over dates and let stand until lukewarm.
3. In the meantime, cream butter, sugar, egg and vanilla together until light and fluffy. Stir in liquid chocolate.
4. Sift flour, salt and baking soda together and then add alternately with date mixture to creamed ingredients. Beat well.
5. Stir in pecans and pour batter (it will be stiff) into prepared loaf pan.
6. Bake at 350º for 1 hour 10 minutes or until it tests done.* Cool 10 minutes and carefully remove from pan.

*See baking tips.

WHEAT GERM BUTTERMILK PANCAKES

2 dozen   A nice change from plain buttermilk pancakes.

1	cup flour
½	cup wheat germ
1	tablespoon sugar
½	teaspoon baking soda
½	teaspoon salt
1½	cups buttermilk*
2	eggs
2	tablespoons oil or melted shortening
	hot griddle or large skillet

*For thinner pancakes, use more buttermilk.

1. Measure flour, wheat germ, sugar, soda and salt into a bowl. Mix well.
2. Add buttermilk, eggs, and oil. Stir well until blended.
3. Cook on lightly greased hot griddle. Bake until puffy and bubbly, turn and bake on other side.
4. Serve hot with butter and syrup, honey or preserves.

BUTTERMILK PANCAKES

12-15 small cakes   A favorite at our house when we have company for breakfast. Serve with Mother's brown sugar syrup, and bacon or sausage.

1   egg
1   cup buttermilk
7/8 cup flour
½   teaspoon salt
1   teaspoon sugar
¾   teaspoon baking powder
½   teaspoon baking soda
2   tablespoons melted butter
     beater
     griddle or large 12" skillet

1. In a medium bowl, beat egg and buttermilk. Sift or mix dry ingredients together, and then beat into milk mixture. Stir in butter.
2. Cook on a hot griddle or skillet. Serve hot with melted butter and warm syrup on warmed plates

My Father loved these pancakes and so does my Mom — When she comes to visit I try to find the time to make them for her. Of course Bob forces himself to eat them!

MOTHER'S BROWN SUGAR SYRUP

Serve on pancakes or rice patties. This stores beautifully in the refrigerator, indefinitely.

1   (1 pound) box of brown sugar
½   cup water
1   teaspoon vanilla

1. In a saucepan, mix sugar and water together. Bring to a boil and simmer mixture until smooth and somewhat thick (5 minutes). Add vanilla.
2. Serve hot or store in a jar in the refrigerator.

I grew up on this homemade syrup and really prefer it to real Vermont Maple Syrup & now have you checked the price difference!

DELUXE POPOVERS

6-8 popovers   A perfect brunch dish, or as a meal accompaniment that is nourishing, too! They will reheat but are best out of the oven.

3   *eggs, room temperature*
1   *cup milk, room temperature*
2   *tablespoons oil*
½   *teaspoon salt*
1   *cup sifted flour*
    rotary beater or wire whip
6-8 *oven proof cups*

1. Preheat oven to 450⁰. Arrange racks.
2. Grease well 8 (5 oz.) custard cups or oven proof cups.
3. In a medium bowl beat eggs, milk, oil and salt thoroughly.
4. Sift flour over egg mixture and beat until just smooth.
5. Pour batter into prepared cups, filling each one half full.
6. Place cups on a baking sheet and bake in the lower half of the oven for 40-45 minutes, until golden brown. After 20 minutes, reduce heat to 350⁰ to prevent over-browning.
7. During the last five minutes, poke popovers with a fork or a knife, for dryer insides. Serve hot with butter and jam.

YORKSHIRE PUDDING

Popover ingredients, but eliminate oil
beef fat for pan (suet)
8 or 9" cast iron skillet

1. Preheat oven to 425⁰.
2. Melt beef fat in the skillet until it is well coated (1-2 tablespoons). Remove fat piece.
3. Prepare popover batter and pour into skillet. Immediately bake at 425⁰ for 30-35 minutes, until brown and firm. (Batter will rise on the side and have a hole in the center.)
4. Cut in slices and serve.

SPECIAL DESSERTS

The paradox in the American Diet today is most interesting. On one hand there is a serious taboo against eating red meats, eggs, sugar, whole milk and fat in the diet. On the other hand, we are increasing our consumption of extra rich ice creams, fancy chocolates or running to fast food operations that specialize in butter rich croissants or fried chicken.
VERY INTERESTING!

"REFRIGERATOR" VANILLA ICE CREAM

TIP: If you have added fruit or cookies you will need a small container to hold extra ice cream since cube tray will be too small for the whole mixture.

3-4 cups

This can be made in the freezer section of your refrigerator, without an ice cream machine. It's really good and the variations are delicious, too.

½ cup sugar
 dash of salt
1 tablespoon flour
¾ cup evaporated milk*
¼ cup water
1 cup heavy cream
1 tablespoon vanilla
 hand beater
 ice cube tray without divider**
 plastic wrap

*You must use evaporated milk to get smooth ice cream.
**Best pan to freeze in for small ice crystals.

1. In a saucepan, mix thoroughly sugar, salt and flour. Blend in milk and water, well.
2. Cook mixture on medium heat until it boils, stirring constantly. Boil one minute. Remove from heat.
3. Pour hot mixture into a medium mixing bowl. Cool for a few minutes and then place in freezer for about one hour.
4. When mixture has begun to freeze, beat heavy cream and vanilla until just stiff. (Don't overbeat.)
5. Remove mixture from freezer and beat (with the same beater) until smooth and aerated.
6. Fold in whipped cream and place bowl back in freezer. (At this time, add fruit, flavors—see variations.)
7. Freeze mixture for about ½ hour. Stir well to blend and pour into the freezer tray. Cover with plastic wrap and freeze until firm. (See Tip)

Variations
Fresh Berry, Peach, Banana—Blend in 1½ cups well-mashed fruit at step 6.

Nut Brittle—Blend in 1 cup crushed nut brittle candy at step 6.

Coffee—Add 1 tablespoon instant coffee to boiling milk sauce.

Chocolate—Stir into hot sauce 1 or 2 (1 oz.) squares melted chocolate.

Cookies 'n Cream—Blend in 1 cup crushed oreo cookies at step 6.

Mint Chip—Blend in ½ cup chocolate chips and a drop of mint extract.

Pistachio—Blend in ½ cup chopped nuts, ½ teaspoon almond extract and a few drops of green food coloring.

HOMEMADE STRAWBERRY ICE CREAM

More like a rich sherbet. This is the best "ice cream" I've ever had. My son in law, Ron, is my biggest fan. Substitute peaches, if you prefer.

5   cups whole strawberries, washed, hulled, drained
1   lemon, juiced
2   cups sugar
4   eggs, separated*
⅔   cup sugar
2   teaspoons vanilla
2   cups cream
    milk for filling
    electric mixer
3   quart freezer

*See egg tips.

1. Puree or finely mash strawberries.
2. In a large bowl, mix strawberries, lemon juice and sugar.
3. Separate eggs. Beat egg whites with ⅓ cup of sugar and vanilla until stiff.
4. In another bowl, beat egg yolks with ⅓ cup sugar until light. Blend into strawberries and add cream.
5. Fold in beaten egg whites and pour mixture into ice cream can. Add milk to finish filling to ⅔ full, if necessary.
6. Churn according to manufacturer's directions. Enjoy!

AUDREY'S FRUIT COBBLER

So easy, and you can vary the fruit. It is good hot with ice cream or whipped cream.

6   tablespoons (¾ cube) butter, melted
1   cup sifted flour
1   cup sugar
½   teaspoon salt
2   teaspoons baking powder
⅔   cup milk
1   large bag of frozen berries or 2-3 cups fresh
½   cup sugar
    ice cream or whipped cream
    flat baking dish 13 X 9"
    wire whip

This dessert seems to get done in more like 30-45 minutes

1. Preheat oven to 350°.
2. Put melted butter in the baking dish.
3. Beat flour, sugar, salt, baking powder and milk together.
4. Sprinkle berries over baking dish. Sprinkle remaining sugar over berries.
5. Pour milk mixture over berries and bake at 350° for 45 minutes to one hour, or until set and brown. Serve warm. *

LEMON CAKE PUDDING

Really popular because its light but a tasty way to end a meal.

Serves 4-6

A low-calorie dessert that is very tasty. Best when served with whipped cream.

¼ cup sifted flour
¾ cup sugar
  dash salt
3 tablespoons melted butter or margarine
¼ cup lemon juice
2 teaspoons lemon rind
3 egg yolks*
1 cup milk
3 egg whites*
1½ quart casserole or souffle dish

See egg tips.

This might cook faster especially if your ingredients aren't too cold. The pudding on the bottom should just start to set.

1. Preheat oven to 350°.
2. In a bowl, mix the flour, sugar, salt and butter. Add juice, lemon rind, yolks and milk; blend well.
3. Beat egg whites until fairly stiff and fold into the first mixture. Pour into greased 1½ quart deep casserole or souffle dish.
4. Bake in a 350° oven for 40 to 45 minutes, or until custard on bottom is just set.* Serve warm with whipped cream.

MACAROON SORBET TORTE

Serves 12-15

Easy, pretty and delicious. Great for a large party. Can be made way ahead.

2 cups heavy cream
  (whipped with a little sugar and vanilla)
2-3 dozen "good" coconut macaroon cookies
2-3 pints softened sherbet or sorbet
  raspberry, pineapple or lime
  (at least 2 different flavors and colors)
  flat glass casserole or deep glass bowl

1. Break up cookies and sprinkle one layer over the bottom of the glass dish.
2. Spoon 2 tablespoon-size dollops of softened sorbet on cookies. Drop some whipped cream on mixture.
3. Repeat a layer of cookies and sorbet. Then smooth to blend. Cover entire mixture with a generous layer of prepared whipped cream. Cover with plastic wrap.
4. Freeze until firm and take out of freezer 15 minutes before serving.

CHOCOLATE CREAM CHEESE SOUFFLE

Serves 4-5

Delicious and really foolproof, if a few easy rules are followed.

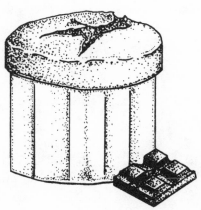

⅓   cup light cream
1   (3 oz.) package cream cheese
½   cup semisweet chocolate chips
3   egg yolks
4   egg whites*
¼   cup sifted powdered sugar
1   quart souffle dish
    clean beating bowl
    wire whip
    whipping cream for topping

*See tips for eggs and souffles.

1. Preheat oven to 325⁰.
2. In a saucepan, blend cream and cream cheese over very low heat. Add chocolate chips and continue to heat until blended. Cool.
3. In a medium bowl, beat egg yolks until thick and lemon colored. Slowly blend cooled chocolate mixture into beaten yolks.
4. In a clean bowl, beat egg whites to soft peaks.* Gradually beat in the powdered sugar until peaks form.
5. Fold in a small amount of whites into the chocolate mixture and then gently blend the whole mixture together, being careful not to over mix.
6. Pour mixture into an ungreased dish and bake in a preheated 325⁰ oven for 50 minutes, or until an inserted knife comes out clean.
7. Serve immediately with whipped cream.

CAROL WALKER'S CHEESE "CAKE"

Serve with fruit topping or fruit sauce. (See sauces.)

Graham Cracker Crust

1¼ cups graham cracker crumbs
¼ cup sugar
6 tablespoons butter or margarine, melted
9" springform pan

1. Preheat oven to 375⁰.
2. Mix everything together and press evenly into pan with 1 to 2 inches up on the sides.
3. Bake in 375⁰ oven for 6-9 minutes, or until edges are just browned.

Filling

4 eggs, beaten
1 cup sugar
1 teaspoon vanilla
 juice of 1 medium lemon
1 (8 oz.) package of cream cheese, softened
 electric beater

1. Beat together all ingredients until smooth. Pour into crust.
2. Bake 25 minutes at 375⁰. Cool for 10 minutes.

Topping

1 cup sour cream
2 tablespoons sugar
1 teaspoon vanilla

1. Heat oven to 475⁰. Mix together sour cream, sugar and vanilla. Spoon on top of "cake."
2. Bake for 5 minutes.
3. Cool and then serve chilled.

MARBLE CHEESECAKE

Serves 12-16   A nice change, but you'll love it.

Crust

> 1½ cups graham cracker crumbs
> ¼ cup sugar
> 6   tablespoons butter, melted
>   9" springform pan

1. Combine cracker crumbs, sugar and butter.
2. Press on the bottom and 2" up the sides of a 9" springform pan. Set aside.

Filling

> 4   (8 oz.) packages cream cheese, softened
> 2   teaspoons vanilla
> 1¾ cup sugar
> 6   eggs
> 2   cups light cream (half and half)
> 2   (1 oz.) squares unsweetened chocolate, melted
>   electric mixer

1. Preheat oven to 450⁰.
2. Beat cream cheese and vanilla until fluffy. Gradually beat in sugar.
3. Beat in eggs, one at a time, until blended. Blend in cream.
4. Combine about 3 cups of the batter with cooled chocolate. Set aside.
5. Pour remaining cheese mixture into prepared crust. Gradually add chocolate mixture using zigzag motion.
6. Bake in 450⁰ oven for 15 minutes, then reduce heat to 300⁰. Continue baking for 1 hour and 10 minutes or until knife inserted halfway between center and edge comes out clean. Cool 1 hour. Remove sides of pan. Chill cake before serving.

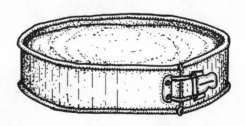

CREPES CHEZ KARLIN

Serves 6

A combination of winning recipes. One of my best ever dessert recipes.

1   dozen crepes (see egg section)
1   recipe raspberry-blueberry sauce, warmed (see sauce recipes)
1   cup heavy cream
1   (3 oz.) package cream cheese, softened
¼   cup powdered sugar
1   teaspoon vanilla
    electric mixer

1. In a deep bowl, beat heavy cream until it is just thick (not stiff).
2. With the same beaters, beat cream cheese, sugar and vanilla. Blend with whipped cream until just smooth.
3. Spread approximately 2 tablespoons of filling on one side of cool crepes. Roll up and chill.
4. At serving time, place 2 crepes on each plate, and top with some warm sauce.

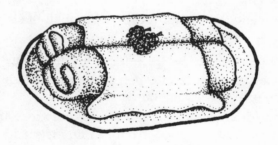

PIES

PASTRY TIPS

The basic recipe used is a standard crust made with only solid shortening, rather than butter and egg combinations. I found I get better results with students with this recipe.
Remember, lots of experience is the best teacher.

EQUIPMENT NEEDS
1. A *glass* or ceramic pie plate with a *flat lip*. Glass will absorb heat and help brown and cook the crust. Metal reflects heat and hinders a good crust.
2. A stocking for the rolling pin and a pastry cloth will make rolling easier and keep the pastry from sticking.
3. A pastry blender, rather than 2 knives.
4. Dry measures to measure flour and shortening accurately.

PASTRY MUSTS
1. Don't substitute ingredients, unless you don't mind different results. Solid "plastic" shortening gives a shorter, flaky crust, while butter gives a better flavor and color.
2. Always sift flour and measure by lightly spooning into measure and then leveling off. *Never pack.*
3. Don't overdo the cutting in step. The "pea" like uneven particles give your pastry the flaky texture.
4. Use ice water to keep the shortening solid. Too much water will toughen the pastry–too little causes the dough to crumble and fall apart.
5. Pastry needs a light hand *except* when attaching and forming the edge on the pie pan.
6. Avoid re-rolling pastry except for leftovers to be used for decorations.

I think my pies & cobblers are my claim to fame

SINGLE PASTRY CRUST

TIP: Pastry can be refrigerated or frozen and then baked when you need it.

Use for all your pies and quiches that need a single crust.

1⅓ cups sifted flour
½ teaspoon salt
½ cup solid shortening (Crisco)
3 tablespoons ice water
  (have a glass of ice water available)
  extra flour
  9″ glass pie pan
  pastry equipment*

See pastry tips.

1. Preheat oven to 425⁰.
2. Put sifted and carefully measured flour into a mixing bowl. Stir salt into flour.
3. With a pastry blender or two knives, "cut in" shortening into flour until mixture is fairly coarse, and resembles small peas or beans. *Do not cut too small.**
4. Sprinkle mixture with 1 tablespoon of water at a time. Toss gently with a fork. Continue to add the rest of the water—3 tablespoons total—until pastry will hold together in a firm ball. (Only add what water is necessary. You may need to sprinkle some into the bowl with your fingers.)
5. On lightly *floured pastry cloth* press dough into a circle about 1″ thick. Begin rolling out dough, but pinch in seams that form and patch holes so dough will not have "inlets" that form. If dough sticks as you roll it, gently lift and rub some flour on the cloth where it is sticking. Roll out to about 1/4″ to 1/8″ thick and 1½″ larger than a 9″ pie pan.
6. *Gently roll* the finished dough onto the rolling pin and then roll well centered into the empty pie pan. *Do not stretch into pan.*
7. *Firmly* flute edge of dough to make a neat edge on the lip of the pie pan. Press pastry firmly to the edge so pastry can have a handle to hold to.* (This also prevents the edge from falling over or down into the pie pan when pastry bakes and expands.)
8. *Baked without filling.* Prick bottom and sides thoroughly with a fork. Chill slightly, then bake at 425⁰ for 10-15 minutes or until just brown. Watch carefully.
9. *Baked with filling.* (Quiches, etc.) Do not prick. Chill and bake according to filling recipe.

*See pastry tips.

DOUBLE PASTRY CRUST

Use this for cherry, apple, berry or any recipe that needs a double crust.

2   *cups sifted flour*
1   *teaspoon salt*
¾   *cup solid shortening (Crisco)*
¼   *cup ice water (approximately)*
    extra flour
    prepared filling
    9" glass pie pan
    pastry equipment*

*See pastry tips.

1. Put sifted and carefully measured flour into a large mixing bowl. Stir salt and flour.
2. With a pastry blender or two knives, "cut in" shortening into flour until mixture is coarse and resembles small peas. (Do not cut too small.)
3. Sprinkle mixture with 1 tablespoon of water at a time. Toss gently with a fork, trying to distribute water throughout. Continue to add the rest of the water—4 tablespoons total—until pastry will hold together in a firm ball. (Only add what water is necessary. You may need to sprinkle some into the bowl with your fingers.)
4. Cut dough not quite in half, and wrap or cover smaller half.
5. On a lightly floured pastry cloth, press larger ball of dough into a circle about 1" thick. Begin rolling out dough, but pinch in seams that form and patch holes so dough will not have "inlets" that form. If dough sticks as you roll it, gently lift and rub some flour on the cloth where it is sticking.
6. Continue to roll until it is about 1/8" thick and 1½" larger than a 9" pie pan. Gently roll the bottom crust onto the rolling pin and then roll into the empty pie pan.
7. Gently ease the crust into the pan and trim the edge if necessary, but allow at least 1" of pastry to overhang the edge.
8. Repeat with the top crust, but you will not need to roll quite as large—only ¾" larger than the pie pan.
9. Fill the bottom crust and put the top crust over the filling. Roll bottom crust *over top* crust edge and crimp edge together firmly. (Moisten layers with some water, if necessary.)
10. Flute pastry and attach *firmly to pan edge.* Cut steam vents on top of pie and bake as directed according to pie filling.

QUICK PIE CRUST

Use the food processor for this easy butter recipe or use standard pastry procedure if you do not have a processor.

1   cube unsalted butter (cut up)
1   cup sifted flour
1   teaspoon sugar
½   teaspoon salt
2   tablespoons ice water
    food processor

1. In the bowl of a food processor, combine cut up butter and dry ingredients. Process until mixture resembles coarse meal. (Don't overdo.)
2. Drip in water and process on and off until dough pulls away from bowl and just starts to form a ball.
3. Remove from bowl and knead with hands once or twice. Wrap and use when needed.*

*See pastry tips for rolling instructions.

CREAM CHEESE PASTRY

Good for 9" pie crust or 24 appetizer tarts.

½   cup butter
1   (3 oz.) package cream cheese, at room temperature
1¼ cup sifted flour
¼   teaspoon salt
    electric mixer or food processor

1. In a large bowl, blend butter and cream cheese with electric mixer.
2. Add flour and salt, all at once, and beat at low speed, or process, just until mixture leaves the sides of bowl and forms ball. Roll out as for single crust.

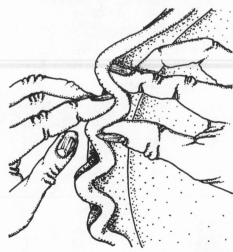

I've discovered that this is a real Favorite

LEMON MERINGUE PIE

This is the best lemon pie I've ever tasted. It can be made in the microwave oven, except the crust, which should be baked conventionally.

TIP: Preheat oven for meringue when filling is cooked.

1   9'' baked pie shell*
1½   cups sugar
6   tablespoons cornstarch
¼   teaspoon salt
½   cup cold water
1   teaspoon grated lemon peel
½   cup fresh lemon juice
3   egg yolks, well beaten (save whites for meringue**)
2   tablespoons butter or margarine, softened
1½   cups boiling water

      *See pastry tips.
      **See egg tips.

1. In a saucepan (glass bowl for microwave) mix sugar, cornstarch and salt and beat with a wire whip until smooth.
2. Gradually blend in cold water, lemon rind and juice. Blend in yolks and butter.
3. Slowly stir in boiling water; gradually bring mixture to a boil over medium heat, stirring constantly. Boil for at least one minute (for microwave, bring mixture to a boil, stirring every 30 seconds. Boil for 1 minute.)*
4. Prepare meringue. (See below.)
5. Pour hot filling into cooled pie shell and cover filling with meringue, making sure that meringue is sealed to crust edge.
6. Bake at 425º for 8-10 minutes, or until golden brown.
7. Cool away from drafts and allow 2 hours before serving.

I made this pie for New Years Eve dinner for the Zupan's in our home in Oregon. I cooked Prime Rib, Yorkshire Pudding & Creamed spinach of course!

Well they took most of the leftover pie home and I saved one piece for me. which my very grown son Jeff consumed the next day.

Next time I'll make a whole pie just pour moi

Meringue

3   egg whites, at room temperature**
¼   teaspoon cream of tartar
      drop of vanilla
6   tablespoon sugar

1. With a mixer, beat egg whites, cream of tartar and vanilla until they barely hold shape.
2. While beating egg whites, add sugar gradually, one tablespoon at a time. Beat at high speed until soft peaks are well formed and sugar is completely dissolved. *Microwave meringue* for approximately 4 to 5 minutes. Brown meringue topping under the broiler for 1 minute if desired. *or carefully put in a hot oven (450°) for a few minutes till brown.*

LEMON CLOUD PIE

6-8 servings   A prize winner from 25 years ago. This is for people
who would love lemon pie without the meringue.
Easy to make in a microwave. Pretty garnished with
whipped cream.

1 (9") baked pie shell
1 cup sugar
4 tablespoons cornstarch
1 cup water
1 teaspoon grated lemon peel
⅓ cup lemon juice
2 eggs, separated
1 (3 oz.) package of softened cream cheese
   electric mixer

1. In a saucepan (glass bowl for microwave), combine ¾ cup of the
   sugar, cornstarch, water, lemon peel, juice and slightly beaten egg
   yolks. Mix well.
2. Cook over medium heat, stirring constantly until the mixture becomes
   thick and boils. Remove from heat and blend in softened cream
   cheese until smooth. Cover and set aside.
3. Using an electric mixer, beat egg whites until frothy. Gradually add
   ¼ cup of the remaining sugar to the whites. Continue to beat until
   they will hold stiff peaks.
4. Fold whites into slightly cooled lemon mixture and pour filling into
   cooled baked pie shell. Chill until set (2-4 hours).

FRESH STRAWBERRY PIE

Serves 6   Should be served the day it is made—and with
whipped cream.

9" baked pie shell, cooled
3-4 boxes strawberries, washed, hulled, drained
1 cup sugar
3 tablespoons cornstarch
   dash of salt
1 tablespoon of lemon juice
   whipped cream

1. Mash about 1 box of ripest prepared strawberries. (Leave the prettiest
   and largest berries whole for the pie.)
2. In a saucepan, blend the sugar, cornstarch, salt and mashed berries.
   Heat on medium, stirring constantly until mixture is thick, bubbly and
   clear. Boil for one or two minutes. Add lemon juice and cool. When
   cool, pour ¼ of "glaze" on bottom of baked pie shell.
3. Arrange whole strawberries in pie shell. Spoon remaining glaze over
   berries so all berries are covered.
4. Chill until glaze is set up. Serve with whipped cream.

MICROWAVE PUMPKIN PIE

A must at Thanksgiving and Christmas dinners

Serves 6-8

This gets more raves than normal pumpkin pie because this method prevents a soggy crust and the filling is delicious.

baked 9" pie shell in a glass pan*
1½ cups pumpkin
1 cup evaporated milk
¾ cup sugar**
2 eggs
¼ teaspoon salt
½ teaspoon cinnamon
½ teaspoon nutmeg
1 teaspoon vanilla
1 tablespoon flour
whipped cream (for topping)

*You must use glass in the microwave.
**⅓ cup brown sugar and ⅓ cup white sugar may be substituted.

TIPS: Cooking time must be adjusted depending on microwave unit.

Sorry, you need a microwave for this, although I'm sure you could use the filling in an *unbaked* shell and bake it conventionally for 30-40 minutes at about 450° until knife pulls clean 1" off center.

1. Blend pumpkin and milk in a large glass bowl. Microwave for 4-5 minutes or until very hot. Stir at least every 30-60 seconds.
2. In a large bowl beat sugar, eggs, salt and spices. Beat hot pumpkin mixture into eggs so it is completely blended.
3. Sprinkle 1 tablespoon of flour on baked pie shell. Pour pumpkin mixture into pie shell.
4. Microwave for 8-9 minutes on high or until pie is set except in the very center. (Knife should pull clean 1" off center.)
5. Cool and serve with whipped cream if desired.

At Xmas I make 2 of these for our crowd. One year my Mom insisted on trying one in a whole wheat crust - Ugh. Then my sister Trudie wanted one made with fructose to try to decrease her sugar intake. After dinner I caught her eating ½ of Helen's white cake and not one bite of pie after all that fuss -

YOGURT CREAM PIE

6-8 servings

Low in calories, rich in flavor.

1 (9") baked pie shell
2 cups blended, flavored yogurt (Not fruit-at-the-bottom type)
1 (9 oz.) container "Cool Whip"
fruit for garnish

1. Blend together yogurt and "Cool Whip" and pour into baked pie shell.
2. Freeze pie, but transfer to refrigerator for a while before serving. Garnish with fruit of your choice.

FRUIT CREAM CHEESE PIE

Serves 6-8   One of the best and prettiest pies ever.

> 1   (9") baked pie shell
> 1   cup whipping cream
> 1   (3 oz.) package cream cheese, softened
> ⅓   cup sifted powdered sugar
> 1   teaspoon vanilla
>   electric beater
>   fruit topping

1. In a medium bowl, beat whipping cream until slightly thickened and begins to hold a shape. Set aside.
2. In a large bowl, beat with same beaters, cream cheese, powdered sugar and vanilla. Add whipped cream and blend well. *Be careful not to overbeat.*
3. Spread mixture evenly into prepared cool crust. Chill until set.
4. Top with desired fruit topping. Chill again until set.

Blueberry Raspberry Topping

> 2   tablespoons cornstarch
> ¼   cup sugar
> 1   cup blueberries
> 1   cup raspberries
> 1   tablespoon port wine or brandy

1. In a saucepan, blend cornstarch, sugar and fruit. Heat on medium heat until thick and boiling. Blend in wine and chill well.
2. When chilled, carefully spread on cream cheese filling.
3. Chill until set and pie will slice easily.

CATHY'S CHOCOLATE CHEESECAKE PIE

Serves 8   This was an experiment by a very special student (another Santa Monica teacher). It has received rave reviews over the years.

> 1   9" chocolate crumb crust
> 1   (8 oz.) package cream cheese, softened
> ½   cup mayonnaise
> ½   cup sugar
> 2   eggs
> 1   6 oz. package semi sweet chocolate chips, melted
> 1   teaspoon vanilla
>   whipped cream for topping
>   electric mixer

1. Preheat oven to 350⁰.
2. In a medium bowl, beat together cream cheese and mayonnaise until smooth.
3. Beat in sugar and then eggs, one at a time.
4. Beat in melted chocolate and vanilla and pour into prepared crust.
5. Bake in 350⁰ oven for 30-35 minutes, or until set. Chill for 4 hours. Serve with whipped cream.

Chocolate Crumb Crust

     Use for Cathy's cheesecake pie or when you desire a chocolate crust.

> *1½ cups chocolate wafer crumbs*
> *6   tablespoons butter (¾ cube), melted*
> *   9" pie pan*

1. Mix together crumbs and butter. Press evenly into pie pan. Chill.

GRANDMOTHER'S CHERRY PIE

     My grandmother lived to be 96 and this was one of her recipes.

> *   double crust pastry**
> *4   tablespoons cornstarch*
> *1½ cups sugar*
> *1/8 teaspoon salt*
> *2   (1 lb.) cans sour cherries*
> *¼   teaspoon red food coloring*
>
> **See pastry recipe.*

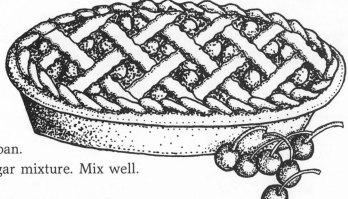

1. Mix together cornstarch, sugar and salt in saucepan.
2. Drain juice from cherries into saucepan with sugar mixture. Mix well. Set cherries aside.
3. Cook juice mixture, stirring constantly, until it boils, thickens and becomes clear. Add cherries and food coloring.
4. Preheat oven to 425⁰.
5. Roll out bottom crust and line 9" pie pan. Roll out top crust and cut about 12 lattice strips for top.
6. Pour cherries into pie shell and lay one layer of lattice strips on filling. Lay second layer of lattice strips at a diagonal. Crimp bottom and strips together to make a nice fluted edge.
7. Bake in 425⁰ oven for 40-45 minutes until crust is brown and filling has bubbled through pie crust.
8. Cool before serving.

APPLE PIE

TIP: For variety, add some apricots, calvados (apple brandy) or raisins.

Serves 6-8

I think this is about the most popular pie of all time. Serve warm with cinnamon ice cream. (See Peach Cobbler.)

double crust pie pastry*
6-8 *green, tart pie apples*
¾-1 *cup sugar (depending on apple tartness)*
3 *tablespoons flour*
1 *teaspoon cinnamon*
¼ *teaspoon nutmeg*
1 *teaspoon vanilla*
dash of salt
2 *tablespoons butter or margarine*
9″ glass pie pan
pastry equipment

*See pastry recipe and tips.

1. Pare apples and slice very thinly.
2. In a large bowl mix sugar, flour, spices and salt. Blend in apples.
3. Roll out ½ of pastry and line pie pan with bottom crust.* Layer apple mixture and dot with butter. Press apples down to compact.
4. Preheat oven to 425⁰.
5. Roll out top crust and place over apples. Roll edges together and flute firmly to pie pan. Cut vent holes for steam to escape.
6. Bake in preheated 425⁰ oven until crust is brown and apples are tender, about 45 minutes. (Mixture should begin to boil.) If crust gets too brown, turn oven down to 350⁰ to finish cooking.
7. Remove from oven and allow to stand until set up.

BERRY PIE

Serves 6-8

Make this with blueberries and peaches or nectarines, if you prefer. This pie is great in the morning for breakfast with a glass of milk.

double crust pie pastry*
3-4 *cups boysenberries, or equivalent*
¾ *cup sugar*
3 *tablespoons flour*
2 *tablespoons butter*
dash cinnamon or nutmeg
9" glass pie pan
pastry equipment*

*See pastry recipe and tips.

1. Roll out ½ of pastry recipe and line pie pan with bottom crust. Fill with fruit.
2. Mix sugar and flour together and sprinkle over fruit. Dot with butter. Add desired spices.
3. Preheat oven to 425⁰.
4. Roll top crust and place over fruit. Roll edges together and flute firmly to pie pan. Cut vent holes for steam to escape.
5. Bake in preheated 425⁰ oven until crust is brown and berry mixture boils thoroughly. (If crust gets too brown, turn oven down to 350⁰ and continue baking.)
6. Remove from oven and allow to cool so filling will thicken and be easier to serve.

FRESH PEACH COBBLER ✳

Serves 8-10

My friend Ruth Ann gave me the idea for this. I changed a few things to make it easier. Use nectarines and blueberries, if you prefer. Serve with cinnamon ice cream.

1 single crust pie pastry
8 to 10 large ripe peaches, peeled and sliced
2-3 tablespoons flour
¾-1 cup sugar
1 teaspoon cinnamon
1/8 teaspoon nutmeg
1 tablespoon lemon juice
2 teaspoons vanilla
3 tablespoons butter or margarine
13 X 9" baking dish
pastry equipment

1. Preheat oven to 425º.
2. Place one layer of sliced peaches into baking dish.
3. Mix flour, sugar, spices, lemon juice and vanilla. Sprinkle some of mixture on peaches.
4. Continue to layer peaches and sugar mixture. Dot with butter.
5. Roll out single crust pastry into a 14 X 10" rectangle. Place crust on top of fruit and flute an edge that is firmly mounted to dish edge.
6. Bake at 425º for 25-30 minutes, or until crust is brown, fruit is just tender and juice mixture is boiling. Serve warm with cinnamon ice cream.

Cinnamon Ice Cream

1 pint vanilla ice cream, softened
1 teaspoon vanilla
½ teaspoon cinnamon

1. In a bowl, stir softened ice cream with vanilla and cinnamon. Freeze until you need it.

✳ My dear friend Lisa says that "my best" is the mixed berry cobbler I make. I use a combination of available berries fresh or frozen raspberries, black berries, blueberries + even some peaches. Adjust the amounts of sugar, flour & spices depending on the amounts and tartness of fruit.

CAKES, COOKIES & CANDIES

CAKE TIPS

1. Prepare pans ahead by greasing with *solid shortening,* flouring, and in many cases, lining pans with waxed paper.
2. Ovens should be preheated and racks arranged so pans do not touch and air circulation is unrestricted.
3. Never substitute ingredients, like cake flour, large eggs,or measure carelessly – unless you enjoy failure.
4. Add ingredients in order and use the proper technique recommended for mixing. Creaming, for example, is very important to the texture of a cake.
5. Never remove a cake from the oven until it tests done.
   • It should pull away from the side of the cake pan.
   • A toothpick should come clean, inserted in the center of the cake.
   • When touched with your finger, the fingerprint should not remain.

COOKIE TIPS

1. Shiny cookie sheets help cookies bake and brown more evenly.
2. Always preheat your oven and bake only one sheet at a time for evenly baked cookies.
3. Always try to test one cookie before baking the whole batch, to make sure they are the right size and consistency. (This is obviously not possible with bar cookies.)
4. Do not substitute or add ingredients, such as honey, flour, or margarine for shortening, unless you like surprises.
5. Bar cookies are done when a fingerprint impression remains in the dough, but a toothpick comes out clean.
6. Most cookies will still be soft when done. Watch closely for color change. Even a minute can make a difference in over-browning.

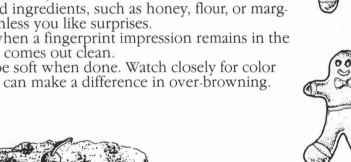

APPLE CAKE

I got this recipe from my mother and it is really well liked. It's good warm or cold.

2 cups flour, sifted
2 cups sugar
2 teaspoons cinnamon
1 teaspoon baking soda
1 teaspoon salt
3 large eggs
1 cup oil
1 teaspoon vanilla
4 cups green apples, peeled and thinly sliced
¾ cup nuts (optional)
   9 X 13 X 2" pan

1. Preheat oven to 350⁰ and grease and flour pan.
2. On paper, sift together all dry ingredients.
3. In a large bowl, beat eggs, oil, and vanilla until foamy. Blend in dry ingredients.
4. Fold in sliced apples and nuts. (Mixture will be very stiff.)
5. Pour mixture into prepared pan and bake at 350⁰ for 55 minutes, or until cake is set and tests done.
6. Partially cool, then ice with cream cheese topping, so cake has a thin coating over entire surface.

Cream Cheese Topping
1 (3 oz.) package cream cheese
3 tablespoons butter
1½ cups powdered sugar
1 teaspoon vanilla

1. Beat cream cheese and butter until creamy. Add sugar and vanilla and beat until smooth.

Extra Special If you really want to go overboard, and not worry about the calories, serve iced cake with the below topping, too.

1 cup whipped cream
1 cup sour cream
1 tablespoon sugar
1 teaspoon vanilla
   cinnamon for sprinkling

1. Gently mix whipped cream, sour cream, sugar and vanilla together.
2. Keep chilled and top warm cake with cream mixture and a sprinkle of cinnamon.

EASY APPLESAUCE CAKE

Quick and easy for those of us who like spice cakes. Vary the spices according to your taste. Good with lemon cream cheese icing.

1   cup applesauce
½   cup oil
4   large eggs
1   teaspoon cinnamon
1   teaspoon pumpkin pie spice
1   teaspoon vanilla
1   cake mix—white or yellow
1   pkg vanilla pudding
     bundt pan or 9 X 13" pan
     electric mixer or wire whip

1. Preheat oven to 350º.
2. Grease and flour bundt pan or cake pan.
3. In a large mixing bowl, add all the ingredients together. Beat with electric mixer 3 to 4 minutes.
4. Pour into prepared pan and bake at 350º for about one hour or until cake tests done.*
5. Cool on rack 5 to 10 minutes. Carefully remove cake from bundt pan (leave in flat pan). Frost when cool, if desired.
*See baking tips.

Lemon Cream Cheese Icing
1   (3 oz.) package cream cheese
2   tablespoons butter
1-2 cups powdered sugar
1   teaspoon vanilla
1-2 tablespoons fresh lemon juice

1. In a small bowl, beat together all ingredients until smooth—adjusting sugar and juice to desired consistency.

AUDREY'S CARROT CAKE

My former next door neighbor was a fabulous coo
who always brought me samples. Of all carrot cakes
I think this version wins the prize. This cake freezes
beautifully if wrapped well. Par-freeze first and then
wrap so icing won't stick to plastic or foil.

2	cups sugar
1¼	cups oil
4	large eggs
2	cups sifted flour
2	teaspoons soda
2	teaspoons cinnamon
1	teaspoon salt
1	teaspoon vanilla
3	cups peeled, grated carrots
½	cup chopped nuts (optional)
	greased 13 X 9" pan or 2 layer pans*

*Please refer to baking tips because success of cake
depends on following the rules exactly.

1. Preheat oven to 300° and grease and flour cake pan.
2. In a large bowl, beat sugar, oil and eggs together till foamy.
3. Sift together flour, soda, cinnamon and salt. Blend the dry ingredient
   into the egg mixture until smooth.
4. Fold in the vanilla, carrots and nuts until blended.
5. Pour into the prepared pan and bake at 300° for 50 to 60 minutes, or
   until the cake tests done.*
6. Cool and frost with cream cheese frosting.

Cream Cheese Frosting

1	(8 oz.) package cream cheese, softened
1	box powdered sugar (sifted)
¼	cup butter (½ cube)
2	teaspoons vanilla

1. Beat all the ingredients together until smooth and creamy. Carefully
   spread on cake.

17 MINUTE FUDGE CAKE

This is so easy but so good, that even chocolate haters will be tempted.

2 cups sugar
2 cups sifted flour
¼ cup unsweetened cocoa
1 cup butter or margarine (2 cubes)
1 cup water
½ cup buttermilk or sour milk
1 teaspoon baking soda
2 eggs
1 teaspoon vanilla
jelly roll pan (15½ X 10½ X 1")

1. Grease jelly roll pan and preheat oven to 400°.
2. Mix sugar and flour in a large mixing bowl.
3. In a medium saucepan, mix cocoa, butter and water. Heat on medium until it begins to simmer.
4. While cocoa mixture is heating, blend buttermilk, soda, eggs and vanilla together.
5. As soon as mixture boils, blend it with the flour and sugar. Blend in milk and egg mixture and beat well.
6. Pour into prepared pan and bake in the preheated 400° oven for exactly 17 minutes.
7. While cake is baking, prepare the frosting.

Frosting

½ cup butter or margarine
6 tablespoons milk
¼ cup cocoa
1 (1 lb.) box powdered sugar
2 teaspoons vanilla
½ cup coarsely chopped walnuts

1. In the same saucepan used for the cake, combine butter, milk and cocoa. Bring to a simmer and remove from heat.
2. Stir in box of sugar, nuts and vanilla until smooth.
3. About 5 to 10 minutes after cake is removed from the oven, begin to ice the cake. Drop spoonfuls of frosting around on cake and carefully spread evenly over entire surface.

BITTERSWEET CHOCOLATE TWEED CAKE

Serves 10-12   A fabulous cake that is very different.

½ cup butter (1 cube)
½ cup sugar
2 cups sifted cake flour
2½ teaspoons baking powder
    pinch of salt
1 cup milk
1 teaspoon vanilla
3 (1 oz.) squares unsweetened chocolate
2 egg whites (save yolks for frosting)
½ cup sugar
3 (8") cake pans
    electric mixer

1. Grease, flour and line pan bottoms with wax paper.
2. Arrange oven racks and preheat oven to 350⁰.
3. In a mixing bowl, cream butter and sugar with mixer till light and fluffy.
4. Sift cake flour, baking powder and salt together. Add to creamed mixture alternately with milk and vanilla. Beat until smooth after each addition.
5. Finely grate 3 squares of chocolate and blend into batter.
6. With a *clean* beater, beat egg whites until foamy. Gradually beat in ½ cup sugar until whites hold stiff peaks and sugar is dissolved.
7. Fold into batter and pour into three prepared cake pans.
8. Bake at 350⁰ for 20 to 25 minutes, until cake tests done.*
9. Cool on racks and then carefully remove from pans. Remove paper and frost.

*See cake tips.

Butter Cream Icing

¾ cup butter (1½ cubes)
3 egg yolks
2¼ cups sifted powdered sugar
1 teaspoon vanilla
1 oz. square semi-sweet chocolate
1 teaspoon water

1. Beat together butter, yolks, sugar and vanilla until smooth.
2. When cake is cool, frost with icing.
3. Melt chocolate with water and drizzle over frosting to decorate.

HELEN'S DEVIL'S FOOD CAKE

My aunt has been pleasing us with this cake for years. Don't let the ingredients surprise you. The lemon extract is absolutely essential in this cake.

1½ cups sugar
¾ cup shortening
2 (1 oz.) squares unsweetened chocolate, melted
3 eggs, separated
1 teaspoon vanilla
1 teaspoon lemon extract
2¼ cups sifted cake flour
1½ teaspoons baking soda
1½ cups buttermilk or sour milk
2 (9") layer cake pans
   electric mixer
   double boiler

1. Grease, flour and line cake pans with waxed paper.
2. Arrange oven racks and preheat oven to 350⁰.
3. In a large mixing bowl, cream sugar and shortening with electric mixer.
4. Blend in melted chocolate and then beat in egg yolks, one at a time. Add vanilla and lemon extracts.
5. Sift measured flour and soda together, twice. Gently blend, with beater, the flour and milk, alternately, into the batter until all is mixed.
6. In a clean bowl with clean beaters, beat whites until just stiff (not dry) and gently fold into cake batter.
7. Pour into prepared pans and bake at 350⁰ for 30 minutes or until cake tests done.*
8. When cake is done, cool on cake racks for 30-45 minutes, before carefully removing from pans to frost.
   *See cake tips.

Nut Filling

1 tablespoon cornstarch
½ cup sugar
1 cup milk
2 egg yolks
1 cup finely chopped nuts
½ teaspoon vanilla
½ teaspoon lemon extract

1. In a saucepan, blend cornstarch and sugar. Add milk and egg yolks.
2. Cook until thick and just bubbling, stirring constantly.
3. Remove from heat and add nuts and flavorings.
4. Cool and spread between layers.

Please —
When you take the time, energy & money to make a scratch cake

Remember to
① Read cake tips
② Don't substitute ingredients
③ Sift flour
④ Use large eggs
⑤ Follow directions

Thanks

(Continued)

Chocolate Icing

2	(1 oz.) squares of unsweetened chocolate
2	cups powdered sugar
¼	teaspoon cream of tartar
2	egg yolks
¼	cup milk
½	teaspoon vanilla
½	teaspoon lemon extract

1. Melt chocolate in top of double boiler over gently bubbling water. (Water should not touch top pan.)
2. Stir in sugar and cream of tartar.
3. Beat yolks and milk together and stir into chocolate.
4. Cook and stir until thickened.
5. Remove from heat and add flavorings.
6. Beat until frosting changes color and is thick enough to spread.

CHOCOLATE CAKE

An easy scratch cake that is moist and so delicious, and don't let the ingredients fool you—because everyone loves it. It's good with buttercream icing or whipped cream.

3	cups sifted flour
1½	cups sugar
⅓	cup cocoa
2¼	teaspoons baking powder
1½	teaspoons baking soda
1½	cup mayonnaise*
1½	cups water
1½	teaspoons vanilla
	wire whip
	13 X 9" pan

Use only regular mayonnaise—not salad dressing or diet mayonnaise

1. Preheat oven to 350° and grease and flour cake pan.
2. In a large bowl, sift together or mix well all the dry ingredients.
3. Stir in mayonnaise and then add water and vanilla gradually. Mix until ingredients are well blended and smooth.
4. Pour into prepared pan and bake at 350° for 30 minutes or until it tests done.*
5. When cool, frost as desired.
*See cake tips.

HELEN'S WHITE CAKE

Of all my Aunt's cakes, this is my sister Trudi's and my favorite. We like it best with 7-minute icing and lemon filling, but it is even good *plain*.

½   cup shortening
1½ cups sugar
2   cups sifted cake flour
2   rounded teaspoons baking powder
1/8 teaspoon salt
¾   cup milk
¼   cup water
1   teaspoon vanilla
4   egg whites*
    electric mixer
2   9″ layer cake pans

See tips on souffles and eggs.

1. Grease, flour and line pans with waxed paper. Preheat oven to 375⁰.
2. In a large bowl, with the electric mixer, cream the shortening and sugar until light and fluffy.
3. Sift together the measured cake flour, baking powder and salt. Mix milk, water and vanilla together.
4. Beat in flour mixture and liquids, *alternately* to creamed mixture. Beat until smooth.
5. With a super clean beater, beat egg whites until peaks form. Fold into cake batter.
6. Pour batter into prepared pans and bake at 375⁰ for 20 minutes or until they test done. *See cake baking tips.*

Lemon Filling—Makes 1⅓ cups
        ¾   cup sugar
        2   tablespoons corn starch
            dash of salt
        ¾   cup water
        2   egg yolks, slightly beaten*
        1   teaspoon grated lemon peel
        3   tablespoons lemon juice
        1   tablespoon butter or margarine

        Save whites for frosting.

1. In a saucepan, combine sugar, corn starch and salt. Stir in water.
2. Stir in yolks, peel and juice. Cook and stir over medium heat until thickened and bubbly. Boil 1 minute.
3. Remove from heat. Stir in butter. Cool to room temperature before using.

(Continued)

Seven Minute Frosting—Frosts 2 layers
        2   *egg whites*
        1½   *cups sugar*
        ¼   *teaspoon cream of tartar*
        ⅓   *cup water*
             dash of salt
        1   *teaspoon vanilla*
             double boiler
             electric mixer

1. On your work space, place all the ingredients, except vanilla, in the top of the double boiler. Beat one minute at low speed to blend.

2. Place over gently boiling water (pan should not touch water) and cook, beating constantly, until frosting forms stiff peaks, *about 7 minutes*. Do not overcook.

3. Remove from boiling water and add vanilla. Continue to beat (off the heat) until spreading consistency, about 2 minutes.

JODI'S POPPY SEED CAKE

Unusual flavors that are a nice change of pace. To be fancy, serve this topped with whipped cream.

        1   *package yellow cake mix*
        4   *large eggs**
        ½   *cup oil*
        2   *packages instant butterscotch pudding*
        ⅓   *cup poppy seeds*
        1¼   *cups water*
             powdered sugar, optional for top
             well greased and floured Bundt pan*
             electric mixer

        *See baking tips.

1. Preheat oven to 350⁰.
2. Grease and flour the pan.*
3. Place the cake mix in a large mixing bowl. Add the remaining ingredients and beat with electric mixer for 3 minutes until the mixture is smooth.
4. Pour into the prepared pan and bake for 45 minutes or until the cake tests done.*
5. Cool for 10 minutes and then carefully remove the cake from the pan. Dust with powdered sugar, if desired.

   *See cake tips.

SOUR CREAM COFFEE CAKE

Good any time of the day! If you like blueberries, fold ½ cup into the batter before putting into the tube pan.

1   cube butter or margarine
1   cup sugar
2   large eggs
1   teaspoon vanilla
1   cup sour cream
2   cups sifted flour
1   teaspoon baking powder
1   teaspoon baking soda
½   teaspoon salt
    electric mixer
    tube pan with removable bottom*

Topping

¼   cup sugar
½   teaspoon cinnamon
½   cup finely chopped nuts

1. Preheat oven to 350° and grease and flour cake pan.
2. Blend the topping ingredients and set aside.
3. In a large bowl, cream together with the electric mixer the butter and sugar until as fluffy as possible (mixture will seem crumbly).
4. Beat in the eggs, then the vanilla and sour cream until completely blended. (Mixture might look curdled at this point.)
5. Sift the dry ingredients together and then slowly beat into the creamy mixture. Mix until well blended, about 1 minute. *Don't overbeat.*
6. Spoon ½ of the batter into prepared tube pan, then sprinkle ½ of the topping on the batter.
7. Add the remainder of the batter and sprinkle with the remaining topping.
8. Bake at 350° for 45 minutes or until the cake tests done.* Serve warm or reheated.

*See tips on baking.

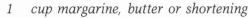

MRS. KARLIN'S OATMEAL CHOCOLATE CHIP COOKIES

TIP: Dough may be refrigerated or frozen and baked when you want fresh cookies.

3 dozen

My daughter Vickie said that her husband didn't like oatmeal cookies, but he sure likes these. Chocolate chips are really a must.

1   cup margarine, butter or shortening
1   cup brown sugar, packed
1   cup white sugar
2   eggs
1½ teaspoons vanilla
1½ cups sifted flour
½   teaspoon salt
½   teaspoon baking soda
½   teaspoon baking powder
3   cups quick cooking oats
¾   cup chocolate chips (optional)
    electric mixer
    cookie sheet

When Rey & Denise come to my house from up North I try to have hot cookies ready for them — Denise seems to have a thing for desserts.

1. Preheat oven to 350º and grease cookie sheet.
2. In a large mixing bowl, cream fat and sugars together until fluffy, with an electric mixer. Beat in eggs and vanilla.
3. Sift measured, sifted flour together with salt, soda and baking powder. Add to creamed mixture and blend well.
4. Stir in oats and chocolate chips. Drop by spoonfuls on greased cookie sheet. Bake in a 350º oven for about 10 minutes, or until they *just* start to brown.
5. Remove hot cookies from sheet immediately and *enjoy*, or cool and store in an airtight container.

CHOCOLATE CREAM CHEESE COOKIES

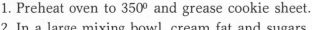

3-4 dozen

This is another one of Mrs. Kellogg's great recipes. The dough freezes well, unbaked. In fact, the baked cookies freeze very well, also. (And, the dough is just delicious—that is, if you're into eating cookie dough.)

½   cup shortening
1½ cups sugar
1   (3 oz.) package cream cheese, softened
1   egg
2   (1 oz.) squares unsweetened chocolate, melted
1   teaspoon vanilla
2¼ cups sifted flour
1½ teaspoon baking powder
2   tablespoons milk
    electric mixer
    cookie sheets

1. Preheat oven to 375⁰.
2. In a large bowl, cream together shortening and sugar until light and fluffy.
3. Beat in cream cheese and egg. Blend in melted chocolate and vanilla.
4. Sift together flour and baking powder. Add flour and milk gradually to dough and beat until just smooth.
5. Drop by small spoonfuls onto a cookie sheet. (You may chill the dough and then roll into balls and flatten, if you prefer a neater cookie.)
6. Bake at 375⁰ for 7 to 8 minutes. Cookies should still be soft to the touch.

COOKIE JAR SUGAR COOKIES

2-3 dozen

These are fun to make with someone else. You should use fancy cookie cutters and then decorate them, especially at Christmas time.

⅔ cup shortening or margarine
¾ cup sugar
1 egg
½ teaspoon vanilla
4 teaspoons milk
2 cups sifted flour
1½ teaspoon baking powder
¼ teaspoon salt
electric mixer
rolling pin
flour and pastry cloth
waxed paper
cookie sheets
cooling racks

Very Important Tip

Don't substitute soft or diet margarine in any baking recipe especially where the dough has to be handled. Butter, hard margarine or shortening work the best.

1. Cream shortening and sugar with electric mixer until fluffy. Beat in egg, vanilla and milk until smooth.
2. Sift measured dry ingredients together and then blend into the creamed mixture until smooth.
3. Wrap dough in waxed paper and chill until the dough can be rolled.
4. When dough can be handled, preheat oven to 375⁰.
5. Cut off about ⅓ of the dough. Roll dough to 1/8" thickness on a floured cloth.
6. Cut in desired shapes and carefully transfer to a greased cookie sheet.
7. Bake in a preheated 375⁰ oven for 6 to 8 minutes, or until cookies just start to brown on the edges. Watch carefully.
8. Remove from sheet immediately and cool on racks. Frost or decorate as desired.
(Continue to roll *chilled* dough or refrigerate dough and bake when desired.)

MOTHER'S BROWN RIM COOKIES

TIP: Remember to test one or two cookies to see how they bake.

5 dozen

Crisp and easy to make. This recipe makes a lot unless, of course, you like to make "elephant" sized cookies. These cookies freeze (baked or unbaked) beautifully, but they are crisp so handle with care as they break easily!

1   cup solid shortening
    (or 1 cube butter and ½ cup shortening)
⅔   cup sugar
1   egg, beaten
1   teaspoon vanilla
½   teaspoon salt
2½ cups sifted flour
¼   cup milk
    electric mixer
    cookie sheet
    drinking glass with flat bottom
    cooling racks

1. Preheat oven to 350⁰.
2. Cream the shortening and sugar together in a mixing bowl until fluffy. Beat in the egg, vanilla and salt.
3. Blend in the flour and the milk until the mixture is very smooth. (Do not over beat.)
4. Drop by spoonfuls onto a lightly greased cookie sheet and press flat with a drinking glass dipped in flour.
5. Bake at 350⁰ for 8 to 10 minutes, or until the cookie edge *just* begins to brown. Remove from the cookie sheet immediately and cool on racks.

CRESCENT TARTS

Makes 3-3½ dozen

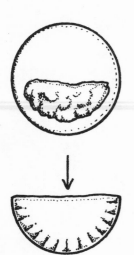

Fill with jam of your choice. These freeze beautifully.

1   cup butter, softened
1   (8 oz.) package of cream cheese, softened
2   cups sifted flour
1   jar of fruit jam
1   beaten egg
    powdered sugar
    3″ biscuit cutter
    pastry cloth—rolling pin
    pastry brush
    cookie sheet

1. In a large bowl, beat together butter and cream cheese. Blend in flour until smooth.
2. Divide dough in half. Wrap and chill until you can handle.
3. When ready to roll, preheat oven to 350⁰.
4. On floured surface or pastry cloth, roll out ½ of the dough to ¼" thickness.
5. Cut circles with floured cutter. Place about ½ teaspoon of jam in the center of each circle.
6. Fold cookies in half and crimp edges with a fork to seal.
7. Carefully place on cookie sheets and brush tops with beaten egg and dust with powdered sugar.
8. Bake at 350⁰ for 15-16 minutes. Remove and cool on rack.

PEANUT BLOSSOMS

3-4 dozen

Delicious peanut butter cookie with a chocolate kiss in the center.

½ cup sugar
½ cup brown sugar
½ cup margarine (1 cube)
1 egg
½ cup peanut butter
2 tablespoons milk
1 teaspoon vanilla
1¾ cups sifted flour
1 teaspoon baking soda
½ teaspoon salt
   sugar for rolling
   48 milk chocolate kisses
   electric mixer
   cookie sheet

1. Preheat oven to 375⁰.
2. In a large bowl, cream sugar, and margarine, using mixer.
3. Beat in egg, peanut butter, milk and vanilla.
4. Sift flour, soda and salt together and blend into first mixture until smooth.
5. Shape into small balls, the size of rounded teaspoons, and roll in sugar.
6. Place on ungreased cookie sheet and bake at 375⁰ for 10 to 12 minutes.
7. Remove cookies from oven and immediately top each cookie with a chocolate kiss. Press kiss into cookie, so that the edges of the cookie crack. Cool on racks.

MRS. KELLOGG'S PINWHEEL COOKIES

TIP: These freeze well before or after baking. Store in cans or air tight containers and label *"No one can eat except the teacher, for fear of death!"*

One of the things I really miss about teaching is that no one makes these cookies for me any more!

3-4 dozen

I always con my students into making these, by saying that "whoever makes these for the teacher will get an 'A!' " They are beautiful to look at and great to eat, but they do take some good "rolling" skills.

1	cup shortening
1	cup sugar
1	egg
1	tablespoon vanilla
3	cups sifted flour
1	teaspoon baking powder
¼	teaspoon salt
5	tablespoons milk
2	(1 oz.) squares unsweetened chocolate, melted

electric mixer
waxed paper or plastic wrap
rolling pin
cookie sheets

1. Cream the shortening and sugar until light and fluffy. Beat in the egg and vanilla.

2. Sift together the measured dry ingredients. Blend into the creamed mixture alternately with the milk, until the mixture is very smooth.

3. Divide the dough in half, and blend the melted chocolate into one half. Wrap the dough pieces separately into waxed paper, and chill until the dough can be rolled out.

4. Using the waxed paper or plastic wrap, begin rolling each piece into a *perfect* rectangle that is 1/8" thick. You will need to chill as you go along and the white dough will be softer than the chocolate.

5. When you have two fairly equal, smooth rectangles that are chilled, lay the white layer on top of the chocolate layer. Roll together, (starting from the longest side) *very carefully*, jelly-roll fashion, making sure dough does not split or crack.

6. Chill roll, well wrapped, until you can make *perfect* slices 1/8 to 1/4 inch thick. Slice and place on a greased cookie sheet.

7. *Bake in a preheated 375° oven* for 8 minutes or until the cookies just begin to start to brown on edge. *Watch* carefully. They should not *brown.*

8. Remove onto a cooling rack, *immediately.*

APPLESAUCE SQUARES

24 - 2″ squares An old fashioned recipe that makes me think of autumn, apples, leaves and spices for fall cooking.

¼ cup shortening or margarine
⅔ cup light brown sugar
1 egg
1 teaspoon vanilla
1 cup sifted flour
1 teaspoon baking soda
½ teaspoon salt
1 teaspoon pumpkin pie spice*
1 cup applesauce
½ cup raisins
13 X 9 X 2″ baking pan

*Combination of cinnamon, nutmeg and cloves.

1. Preheat oven to 350⁰. Grease and flour pan.
2. In a bowl, cream shortening and sugar together until fluffy. Beat in egg and vanilla.
3. Sift measured flour, soda, salt and spice together. Blend into creamed mixture. Fold in applesauce and raisins. Mix well.
4. Pour into prepared pan and bake at 350⁰ for 25 minutes.
5. Remove from oven and cool on rack. Frost when fairly cool. Cut into approximately 2″ squares.

Icing

3 tablespoons butter
1½ cup powdered sugar
1 teaspoon vanilla
2 tablespoons milk

1. In a saucepan, heat butter until it just begins to turn light brown. (Do not burn.)
2. Remove from heat and beat in remaining ingredients, until smooth.

SPECIAL LEMON BARS

30-40 squares Probably one of the most popular cookies—that is, if you like lemon. These freeze well after baking.

Crust

½ cup powdered sugar
1 cup butter
2 cups sifted flour
9 X 13″ glass baking pan

1. Preheat oven to 350º.
2. Mix sugar, butter and flour into a dough and pat evenly into the baking pan.
3. Bake at 350º for 15 minutes and remove from oven.

Filling

Be sure and use large eggs or you'll ruin the recipe

4	eggs
2	teaspoons lemon rind
5	tablespoons fresh lemon juice
2	cups sugar
1	teaspoon baking powder
4	tablespoons flour
	powdered sugar for top

1. While crust is baking, beat together the eggs, lemon rind, juice, sugar, baking powder and flour.
2. When the crust comes out of the oven, pour the lemon mixture over the crust.
3. Bake an additional 25 minutes at 350º.
4. Remove from the oven and sprinkle with powdered sugar and cool. Cut into 1" squares.

OATMEAL JAM BARS

25-30 bars   Delicious and fairly nutritious. They freeze beautifully after baking, just wrap them well.

The crumb mixture can be used as a cobbler topping in place of pastry.

1⅓	cup sifted flour
¼	teaspoon baking soda
¼	teaspoon salt
¾	cup quick cooking oats
⅓	cup brown sugar
2	(3 oz.) packages softened cream cheese
¼	cup soft butter or margarine
1	teaspoon vanilla
¾	cup jam (boysenberry or apricot)
1	teaspoon lemon juice
	9 X 9 X 2" greased baking pan

1. Preheat oven to 350º and prepare pan.
2. In a mixing bowl, blend together well the flour, soda, salt, oats and sugar.
3. In another small bowl, beat together the cream cheese, butter and vanilla. Cut this mixture into the dry ingredients until the mixture is crumbly and fairly evenly blended. Set aside one cup of crumbs.
4. Pat the remainder of the crumbs into the greased baking pan. Bake in the 350º oven for 20 minutes.
5. Combine jam and lemon juice and spread over the pre-baked crust. Sprinkle the reserved crumbs over the top and bake for an additional 15 minutes or until brown.
6. Cool on a wire rack and then cut into bars.

DREAM BARS

24 - 2" squares   A real favorite at our Christmas party at school.

TIP: If you store tightly covered, cookies will remain fresh for a week.

½ cup butter (1 cube)
1   cup sifted flour
½ cup brown sugar
2   eggs
1   cup light brown sugar
½ teaspoon vanilla
¼ teaspoon baking powder
    dash of salt
1½ cups coconut
1   cup chopped nuts
    flat 9 X 13" baking dish

1. Preheat oven to 350°.
2. Mix butter, flour and brown sugar like a pastry dough and pat evenly over the bottom of the baking pan. Bake at 350° for 10 to 12 minutes or until it is set and just *starts* to brown.
3. Beat eggs, sugar, vanilla, baking powder and salt together. Fold in coconut and nuts and pour over the crust as soon as crust is baked and removed from the oven.
4. Return to the oven and continue baking for 20 minutes or until it is set.
5. Remove from the oven and spread icing evenly over the cookies. Cool and cut into small bars.

Icing

1   tablespoon melted butter
½ lemon—juice and rind
½ small orange—juice and rind
    powdered sugar

1. Mix butter, juice, and rind together. Add enough powdered sugar to make icing like a thick glaze or so it will spread well over the cookies.
2. Make sure that the cookies have some icing, but not too much—just a glaze.

"HOMEMADE" BROWNIES

32 squares

This is my Aunt Helen's recipe. They freeze beautifully, if you have any left over.

1 cup butter or margarine
2 cups sugar
4 eggs, beaten well
2 teaspoons vanilla
4 (1 oz.) squares unsweetened chocolate, melted
1 cup sifted flour
1 cup nuts, chopped (optional)
2 (8 X 8") square pans, greased
   electric mixer

1. Preheat oven to 325°.
2. With mixer, cream butter and sugar until light and fluffy. Beat in eggs and vanilla.
3. Mix in the melted chocolate. Stir in the flour until blended. Add nuts, if desired.
4. Pour into prepared pans and bake 30 to 35 minutes.* (Bar cookies must not be overcooked. They should leave a slight finger indent when touched.
5. Cool and cut into squares.

*See baking and cookie tips.

ROBIN'S ORANGE BLOSSOM SQUARES

24 - 2" squares

Delicious warm but good even from the freezer.

¾ cup soft butter or margarine
1½ cup sugar
2 eggs
1 teaspoon vanilla
2½ cups sifted flour
½ teaspoon salt
2 teaspoons baking powder
½ cup orange juice
1 (6 oz.) package chocolate chips
   greased and floured 9 X 13" pan
   electric mixer

1. Preheat oven to 350⁰ and prepare pan.
2. In a bowl, cream together the butter and sugar with an electric mixer until light and fluffy. **BEAT IN EGGS & VANILLA**
3. Sift flour, salt and baking powder together. Blend into creamed mixture, alternately, with orange juice until smooth.
4. *Fold* in chocolate chips.
5. Pour into prepared pan and bake at 350⁰ for 35 to 40 minutes until it tests done, as a cake should.*
6. Cool and then cover with the prepared glaze.
7. Cut into squares and serve or freeze, if desired.

*See baking tips.

Glaze

> 1½ cups sifted powdered sugar
> 3 tablespoons orange juice

1. Mix powdered sugar and juice until smooth. Pour on cooled cake.

I criticized one of my men students for not adding the eggs in this Recipe. His reply was "but Mrs Karlin your book didn't tell when to add the eggs- so I didn't!"

MOTHER'S HOMEMADE FUDGE

36 pieces

If you like real homemade fudge, you will love this. It's an old fashioned recipe—not foolproof, because any cooked candy recipe can fail just with a change of weather.

TIP: A thermometer is a must for success with candy making.

> 3 cups sugar
> ¼ cup unsweetened cocoa
> ½ cup white Karo syrup
> 1½ cups evaporated milk
> ½ cube (¼ cup) butter
> 1 teaspoon vanilla
> candy thermometer
> buttered 3-4 quart saucepan
> small baking pan

I'll always remember my Mom "yelling" at me when I was little "Don't touch the fudge while it's cooling"

1. In a buttered saucepan, combine the sugar, cocoa, Karo and milk.
2. On medium to medium high heat, bring to a rolling boil—stirring occasionally just to keep blended. *Make sure it does not stick or burn.*
3. Place thermometer in pan and continue to boil until it reaches a soft ball stage, or 236⁰ on the thermometer.*
4. Remove from heat and drop in butter. Set aside and let cool *undisturbed* to 110⁰.
5. When cool, add vanilla and begin beating vigorously till fudge stiffens and loses its gloss.
6. *Quickly* push mixture into small baking pan. Smooth out as much as possible. Cut into squares when set.

*Drop a little candy in some cold water and test to see if it makes a soft ball.

ENGLISH TOFFEE

Must be made in a large skillet, but it's easy and *almost* foolproof.

¾ pound butter (3 cubes)
1½ cups sugar
    large chocolate bar
½ cup chopped nuts
    10-12″ skillet (prefer electric skillet)
    jelly roll pan

1. In the large skillet, melt butter on low heat. Stir in sugar until butter and sugar are well blended.
2. On medium high heat, cook the mixture, stirring constantly until it lightly browns and looks coffee colored—about 20 minutes.
3. Pour into pan and cool.
4. Melt chocolate bar and spread on cooled toffee. Immediately sprinkle with nuts so they adhere to the chocolate. Chill.
5. When chilled, break into desired sized pieces.

SPICY WALNUTS

Delicious and easy to make.

2½ cups walnut halves
1   cup sugar
½   cup water
1   teaspoon cinnamon
½   teaspoon salt
1½ teaspoons vanilla
    buttered saucepan
    candy thermometer

1. In a skillet or 350⁰ oven, heat the nuts (do not brown) for about 5 minutes.
2. In the buttered saucepan, combine sugar, water, cinnamon and salt.
3. Heat on medium high until sugar dissolves and mixture boils. Continue to cook without stirring until mixture reaches soft ball stage or 236⁰.
4. Remove from heat. Beat vigorously until mixture gets creamy—about 1 minute. Stir in vanilla and warm walnuts till nuts are well coated.
5. Turn out on a buttered sheet and separate with two forks.

STOCKS, SAUCES & CONDIMENTS

STOCK TIPS

There seems to be some confusion about the terms stock, broth or bouillon since they are often used interchangeably in recipes. If and when you come across stock or broth in this book or in others please realize that we are referring to the same ingredient.

It is true that a good "stock" is the basis for the best soups and sauces, but because of time most people rely on preprepared ingredients.

If you prefer a homemade white stock you can use BOB'S CHICKEN SOUP recipe or refer to a general cookbook for a brown stock. If you don't have 4 to 6 hours to make homemade stock, use the canned variety or the seasoned stock bases in jars. BEWARE of the extreme saltiness that is common in prepared stock bases and adjust your recipes accordingly.

HERB BUTTER

Delicious on broiled steaks, chops, corn or even bread.

1   cube (¼ lb.) butter, softened
1   small clove of garlic—mashed
1   tablespoon finely minced green onions
1   teaspoon dill weed
1   teaspoon lemon juice
¼   teaspoon Worcestershire sauce
1/8 teaspoon fresh ground pepper
½   teaspoon paprika

1. In a bowl blend all ingredients.
2. Spread 1 tablespoon or so on hot broiled steaks or chops. MMMMMM-Delicious!

MEXICAN "SPANISH" SAUCE

Makes 1½ cups   Great on omelets, fish, chicken, etc.

2   tablespoons olive oil
1   clove garlic, minced
1   onion, chopped
1   (8 oz.) can tomato sauce
½   teaspoon ground cumin
¼   teaspoon salt
    dash pepper
    bay leaf
½   teaspoon marjoram
½   teaspoon chili powder (Gebharts)

1. In a skillet, slowly saute garlic and onion in olive oil. Stir in remaining ingredients and simmer on low heat for 15 minutes.
2. Taste for seasoning and thin with water if desired.

CUCUMBER HERB SAUCE

1½ cups   Great on any fish dish or vegetables.

½   cup sour cream
½   cup peeled, shredded cucumbers
¼   cup plain yogurt
1   teaspoon minced parsley
1   teaspoon chopped chives
½   teaspoon dill weed
1   tablespoon lemon juice
1/8 teaspoon salt

1. Mix all ingredients together and serve chilled.

BOB'S PESTO SAUCE

Serves 4-8

This recipe came from his "new" garden—serve on hot pasta. It freezes very well.

½   cup olive oil
2   cups FRESH basil leaves*
4   sprigs FRESH parsley
2   cloves garlic
1   teaspoon seasoned salt
2   tablespoons pine nuts or almonds
½   cup freshly grated Parmesan cheese

Dry herbs cannot be used.

1. Put oil, basil, parsley, garlic, salt and nuts in a food processor or blender. Blend until everything is finely minced.
2. Stir in cheese and taste for seasoning.

TIP: Blend oil, basil, garlic and salt together and put this mixture in jars. Cover with some oil and it will keep refrigerated for weeks. To complete pesto, just add nuts and parmesan cheese.

PASTA PORTION

1   pound spaghetti or noodles
4   tablespoons butter
    pesto sauce

1. Cook pasta and drain well. Toss with butter and then with desired amount of pesto sauce.
2. Serve immediately with more cheese if desired.

TERIYAKI MARINADE

Delicious on steaks, chicken or whatever you like teriyaki on.

⅔   cup soy sauce
⅓   cup sherry or sweet wine
¼   cup brown sugar
1   teaspoon chopped fresh ginger root
    or ¼ teaspoon ground ginger
2   tablespoons oil
1   garlic clove, minced
1   teaspoon sesame oil (if available)

1. Mix together until well mixed blended in a sauce pan. Heat gently to dissolve sugar and mix flavors.
2. For increased flavor, marinate meat or chicken ahead of time. Cook as desired, basting as you cook.

"HOT" CHOCOLATE SAUCE

Please don't miss this one.

Serves 2-3

My mother made a version of this when we were kids and we loved it because it got chewy on the cold ice cream. It works the easiest if made in the microwave but you must use glass to cook in.

Wonderful when poured over fresh fruit & vanilla ice cream.

¼   *cup unsweetened cocoa*
¼   *cup sugar*
1   *teaspoon vanilla*
2   *tablespoons brewed strong coffee*
1   *quart glass measure*

1. Thoroughly mix cocoa, sugar, vanilla and coffee in the large glass measure or a small heavy saucepan, for stovetop cooking.
2. Bring mixture to a boil and simmer sauce for a few minutes or until it begins to thicken. Be careful that mixture does not boil over if using the microwave. If you use a conventional burner, chocolate should be heated carefully so it does not burn.
3. Pour while hot on ice cream and enjoy.

BLUEBERRY-RASPBERRY SAUCE

A must on Karlin's Crepes, but also delicious on ice cream, or angel cake with whipped cream.

½   *cup sugar*
2   *tablespoons cornstarch*
    pinch of salt
2   *cups mixed blueberries and raspberries**
1   *tablespoon port wine or brandy*

    *May use frozen berries

1. In a saucepan, mix well the sugar, cornstarch and salt. Blend in fruit.
2. Bring to a boil over medium heat, stirring regularly. Boil until thick and clear.
3. Stir in wine and taste. Serve warm over crepes or ice cream.

ORANGE LEMON SAUCE

TIP: Remember to grate the lemon for the peel before you juice it.

Delicious served on crepes, ice cream, or whatever.

⅓   *cup sugar*
2   *teaspoons cornstarch*
    dash of salt
½   *teaspoon finely grated lemon peel*
    juice of one lemon
½   *cup orange juice*

1. In a saucepan, mix well the sugar, cornstarch and salt. Blend in juices and lemon peel.
2. Cook over medium heat, stirring constantly until mixture comes to a boil and becomes clear.

CUCUMBER AND ONION RELISH

This is best made in advance, covered and chilled well.

2   cucumbers
1   onion
1   teaspoon salt
2   tablespoons vinegar
3   tablespoons water
1   teaspoon sugar

1. Score the cucumbers with the tines of a fork. Slice the cucumbers and onion very thinly. Place in a bowl with salt and allow to stand for 30 minutes. Pour off liquid that accumulates.
2. Add vinegar, water and sugar. Chill well before serving.

FRESH CRANBERRY AND ORANGE RELISH

A nice change from canned cranberry sauce. It's delicious when served over sliced, firm pears.

2   cups cranberries
1   small orange
½   cup sugar
    food processor or blender*

1. Wash cranberries. Peel the orange and cut into pieces (remove seeds).
2. Chop the fruit in a food processor or blender.* Add the sugar and blend thoroughly. Let stand at least 30 minutes before serving.

*If using a blender, divide fruit into small batches to blend.

GRANDMA'S PLUM JELLY

Makes 8-10
(8 oz.) jars

Absolutely the best jelly in the world, but I was raised on it, so I am spoiled for anything else.

5 pounds pitted (not peeled) Santa Rosa plums
1½ cups water
7½ cups sugar
1 box Sure Jel pectin
   6-8 quart covered kettle
   8-10 sterilized jars, with new lids
   cheesecloth

1. Finely chop fruit and place in kettle. Add water and cover pan.
2. Bring to a boil and simmer for 10 minutes, stirring occasionally.
3. Place layers of cheesecloth over a bowl and pour simmered fruit into cloth. Squeeze and let drip until 5½ cups of juice have been collected. (Add more water to fruit to obtain enough juice.)
4. Add 5½ cups of juice and pectin back into kettle. Mix well.
5. Bring to a boil, stirring constantly.
6. Stir in sugar and return to a full rolling boil.
7. Remove from heat and pour into prepared jars, leaving 1/8" head space.
8. Seal jar properly with sterilized 2-piece lids.
9. Label and store in a dry, "cool" place.

My Aunt Helen says this is really her recipe. Helen is 85+ now and still making this jam for me every year if she can get the plums for a good price.

MICROWAVE RASPBERRY JAM

Makes 3-4
(8 oz.) jars

Super good and so easy. Substitute one package of frozen blueberries for a nice combination.

2 (10 oz.) packages frozen raspberries
3½ tablespoons powdered fruit pectin
2½ cups sugar
1 tablespoon lemon juice
   large glass mixing bowl
4 sterilized jelly jars

1. In the large bowl, put fruit and pectin. Microwave for 5 to 6 minutes, on high. Stir well.
2. Microwave for 3 to 4 minutes. Stir in sugar and lemon juice.
3. Continue to microwave for 2 to 3 minutes, making sure mixture has boiled well for a minute or so. (Watch and stir during cooking so mixture does not boil over.)
4. Skim, if necessary, and pour into glasses. Refrigerate or cover with paraffin and store properly.

SPECIAL HELPS

EQUIVALENTS & STANDARD MEASURES

Abbreviations

(t) . . . . . . teaspoon
(T) . . . . . tablespoon
(c) . . . . . . cup
(pt) . . . . . pint
(qt) . . . . . quart
(gal) . . . . gallon
(oz) . . . . . ounce
(lb) . . . . . pound
(sq) . . . . . square

Facts to Memorize

3 t . . . . = 1 T
16 T . . . . = 1 c
2 c . . . . = 1 pt
4 c . . . . = 1 qt
4 qt . . . . = 1 gal
8 oz . . . . = 1 c
16 oz . . . . = 1 lb
1 stick butter . . = ½ c

When Cooking Remember

½ c butter . . . . = 1 cube or ¼ lb.
1 lb butter . . . . = 2 c
¼ lb cheese. . . . . = 1 c shredded
4 c flour . . . . = 1 lb
1 lb granulated sugar . . = 2⅓ c
1 lb brown sugar . . . . = 2¼ c packed
1 lb powdered sugar = 3½ c sifted
1 sq chocolate . . . . = 1 oz
1 sq chocolate. . . . . = 3 T cocoa plus 1 T shortening
1 c sour milk . . . . = 1 T vinegar or lemon juice
plus enough milk to equal 1 c
1 c uncooked macaroni = 2 ½ c cooked
4 slices bread . . . . = 1 c bread crumbs

Sam
how I miss you!
you were so
special

FOOD PREPARATION TERMS

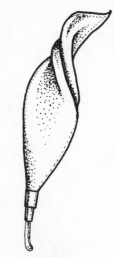

Bake—To cook covered or uncovered in an oven or oven-type appliance. For meats cooked uncovered, it's called roasting.

Baste—To moisten foods during cooking with pan drippings or special sauce to add flavor and prevent drying.

Beat—To make mixture smooth by adding air with a brisk whipping or stirring motion using spoon or electric mixer.

Blanch—To precook in boiling water or steam to prepare foods for canning or freezing, or to loosen skin.

Blend—To thoroughly mix two or more ingredients until smooth and uniform.

Boil—To cook in liquid at boiling temperature (212° at sea level) where bubbles rise to the surface and break. For a full rolling boil, bubbles form rapidly throughout the mixture.

Braise—To cook slowly with a small amount of liquid in tightly covered pan on top of range or in oven.

Bread—To coat with bread crumbs before cooking.

Broil—To cook by direct heat, usually in broiler, or over coals.

Candied—To cook in sugar or syrup when applied to sweet potatoes or carrots. For fruit or fruit peel, to cook in heavy syrup till translucent and well coated.

Caramelize—To melt sugar slowly over low heat until it becomes brown in color.

Chill—To place in refrigerator to reduce temperature.

Chop—To cut in pieces about the size of peas with knife, chopper, or blender.

Cool—To remove from heat and let stand at room temperature.

Cream—To beat with spoon or electric mixer till mixture is soft and smooth. When applied to blending shortening and sugar, mixture is beaten till light and fluffy.

Cut in—To mix shortening with dry ingredients using pastry blender or knives.

Dice—To cut food in small cubes of uniform size and shape.

Dissolve—To disperse a dry substance in a liquid to form a solution.

Dredge—To sprinkle or coat with flour or other fine substance.

Flake—To break lightly into small pieces.

Fold—To add ingredients gently to a mixture. Using a spatula, cut down through mixture; go across bottom of bowl and up and over, close to surface. Turn bowl frequently for even distribution.

Fry—To cook in hot shortening. Panfrying is to cook in a small amount of shortening. Deep-fat frying is to cook immersed in large amount of shortening.

Glaze—A mixture applied to food which hardens or becomes firm and/or adds flavor and a glossy appearance.

Grate—To rub on a grater that separates the food into very fine particles.

Knead—To work the dough with the heel of the hand with a pressing, folding motion.

Marinate—To allow a food to stand in a liquid to tenderize or to add flavor.

Mince—To cut or finely chop food into very small pieces.

Mix—To combine ingredients, usually by stirring, till evenly distributed.

Panbroil—To cook uncovered on hot surface, removing fat as it accumulates.

Panfry—To cook in small amount of hot shortening.

Pit—To remove pits from fruits.

Poach—To cook in hot liquid, being careful that food holds its shape while cooking.

Precook—To cook food partially or completely before final cooking or reheating.

Roast—To cook uncovered without water added, usually in an oven.

Saute—To brown or cook in a small amount of hot shortening.

Scald—To bring to a temperature just below the boiling point where tiny bubbles form at the edge of the pan.

Scallop—To bake food, usually in a casserole, with sauce or other liquid. Crumbs are often sprinkled atop.

Score—To cut narrow grooves or slits part way through the outer surface of food.

Sear—To brown the surface of meat very quickly by intense heat.

Shred—To rub on a shredder to form small, long narrow pieces.

Sift—To put one or more dry ingredients through a sieve or sifter.

Simmer—To cook in liquid over low heat at a temperature of 185° to 210° where bubbles form at a slow rate and burst before reaching the surface.

Soft peaks—To beat egg whites or whipping cream till peaks are formed when beaters are lifted, but tips curl over.

Steam—To cook in steam with or without pressure. A small amount of boiling water is used, more water being added during steaming process if necessary.

Steep—To extract color, flavor, or other qualities from a substance by leaving it in liquid just below the boiling point.

Stew—To simmer slowly in a small amount of liquid.

Stiff peaks—To beat egg whites till peaks stand up straight when beaters are lifted, but are still moist and glossy.

Stir—To mix ingredients with a circular motion until well blended or of uniform consistency.

Toss—To mix ingredients lightly.

Truss—To secure fowl or other meat with skewers to hold its shape during cooking.

Whip—To beat rapidly to incorporate air and produce expansion, as in heavy cream or egg whites.

NUTRITION & DIET TIPS

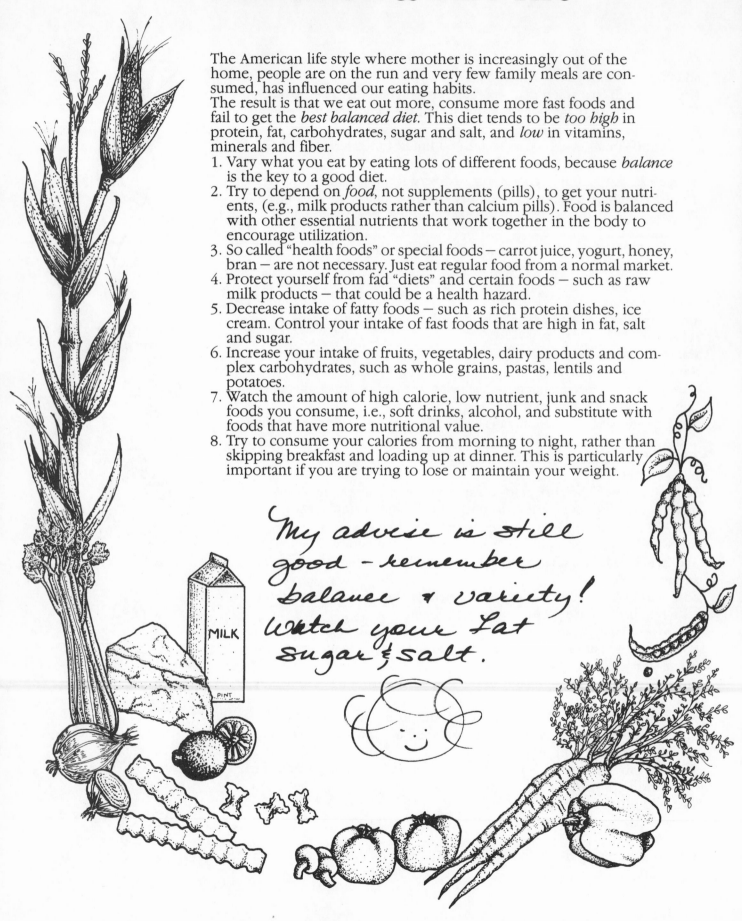

The American life style where mother is increasingly out of the home, people are on the run and very few family meals are consumed, has influenced our eating habits.

The result is that we eat out more, consume more fast foods and fail to get the *best balanced diet*. This diet tends to be *too high* in protein, fat, carbohydrates, sugar and salt, and *low* in vitamins, minerals and fiber.

1. Vary what you eat by eating lots of different foods, because *balance* is the key to a good diet.
2. Try to depend on *food*, not supplements (pills), to get your nutrients, (e.g., milk products rather than calcium pills). Food is balanced with other essential nutrients that work together in the body to encourage utilization.
3. So called "health foods" or special foods — carrot juice, yogurt, honey, bran — are not necessary. Just eat regular food from a normal market.
4. Protect yourself from fad "diets" and certain foods — such as raw milk products — that could be a health hazard.
5. Decrease intake of fatty foods — such as rich protein dishes, ice cream. Control your intake of fast foods that are high in fat, salt and sugar.
6. Increase your intake of fruits, vegetables, dairy products and complex carbohydrates, such as whole grains, pastas, lentils and potatoes.
7. Watch the amount of high calorie, low nutrient, junk and snack foods you consume, i.e., soft drinks, alcohol, and substitute with foods that have more nutritional value.
8. Try to consume your calories from morning to night, rather than skipping breakfast and loading up at dinner. This is particularly important if you are trying to lose or maintain your weight.

My advice is still good — remember balance & variety! Watch your fat sugar & salt.

INDEX

✱ Biscuits page (114)
Cheese Biscuits page (90)

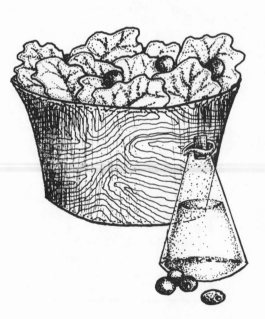

ORDER FORM

Please indicate the number of copies you wish to order on this form and include your check or money order. California residents include 6.25% sales tax, and Los Angeles County residents include 6.75% sales tax. There is a $3.00 shipping and handling charge. (If no order form is available, just use any paper.)

PURCHASER:

_____
NAME

_____
ADDRESS

_____
CITY/STATE/ZIP

Please send _____ copies of KARLIN'S KITCHEN to:

_____
NAME

_____
ADDRESS

_____
CITY/STATE/ZIP

Please send _____ copies of KARLIN'S KITCHEN to:

_____
NAME

_____
ADDRESS

_____
CITY/STATE/ZIP

Please send _____ copies of KARLIN'S KITCHEN to:

_____
NAME

_____
ADDRESS

_____
CITY/STATE/ZIP

I have ordered _____ copies of KARLIN'S KITCHEN @ $14.00 $_____

California Residents 6.25% Sales Tax   ($0.875 ea.)   _____

Los Angeles County Residents 0.5% Sales Tax   ($0.07 ea.)   _____

$3.00 Shipping & Handling per order   3.00

TOTAL ENCLOSED (Round up to nearest penny)   _____

Mail to KARLIN'S KITCHEN, 1343 Sunset Avenue, Santa Monica, California 90405

Autographed gift ideas for family & friends

ORDER FORM

Please indicate the number of copies you wish to order on this form and include your check or money order. California residents include 6.25% sales tax, and Los Angeles County residents include 6.75% sales tax. There is a $3.00 shipping and handling charge. (If no order form is available, just use any paper.)

PURCHASER:

_____
NAME

_____
ADDRESS

_____
CITY/STATE/ZIP

Please send _____ copies of KARLIN'S KITCHEN to:

_____
NAME

_____
ADDRESS

_____
CITY/STATE/ZIP

Please send _____ copies of KARLIN'S KITCHEN to:

_____
NAME

_____
ADDRESS

_____
CITY/STATE/ZIP

Please send _____ copies of KARLIN'S KITCHEN to:

_____
NAME

_____
ADDRESS

_____
CITY/STATE/ZIP

I have ordered _____ copies of KARLIN'S KITCHEN @ $14.00 $_____

California Residents 6.25% Sales Tax   ($0.875 ea.)   _____

Los Angeles County Residents 0.5% Sales Tax   ($0.07 ea.)   _____

$3.00 Shipping & Handling per order   3.00

TOTAL ENCLOSED (Round up to nearest penny)   _____

Mail to KARLIN'S KITCHEN, 1343 Sunset Avenue, Santa Monica, California 90405

ORDER FORM

Please indicate the number of copies you wish to order on this form and include your check or money order. California residents include 6.25% sales tax, and Los Angeles County residents include 6.75% sales tax. There is a $3.00 shipping and handling charge. (If no order form is available, just use any paper.)

PURCHASER:

_____
NAME

_____
ADDRESS

_____
CITY/STATE/ZIP

Please send _____ copies of KARLIN'S KITCHEN to:

_____
NAME

_____
ADDRESS

_____
CITY/STATE/ZIP

Please send _____ copies of KARLIN'S KITCHEN to:

_____
NAME

_____
ADDRESS

_____
CITY/STATE/ZIP

Please send _____ copies of KARLIN'S KITCHEN to:

_____
NAME

_____
ADDRESS

_____
CITY/STATE/ZIP

I have ordered _____ copies of KARLIN'S KITCHEN @ $14.00 $_____

California Residents 6.25% Sales Tax   ($0.875 ea.)   _____

Los Angeles County Residents 0.5% Sales Tax   ($0.07 ea.)   _____

$3.00 Shipping & Handling per order   __3.00__

TOTAL ENCLOSED (Round up to nearest penny)   _____

Mail to KARLIN'S KITCHEN, 1343 Sunset Avenue, Santa Monica, California 90405

ORDER FORM

Please indicate the number of copies you wish to order on this form and include your check or money order. California residents include 6.25% sales tax, and Los Angeles County residents include 6.75% sales tax. There is a $3.00 shipping and handling charge. (If no order form is available, just use any paper.)

PURCHASER:

_____
NAME

_____
ADDRESS

_____
CITY/STATE/ZIP

Please send _____ copies of KARLIN'S KITCHEN to:

_____
NAME

_____
ADDRESS

_____
CITY/STATE/ZIP

Please send _____ copies of KARLIN'S KITCHEN to:

_____
NAME

_____
ADDRESS

_____
CITY/STATE/ZIP

Please send _____ copies of KARLIN'S KITCHEN to:

_____
NAME

_____
ADDRESS

_____
CITY/STATE/ZIP

I have ordered _____ copies of KARLIN'S KITCHEN @ $14.00	$_____
California Residents 6.25% Sales Tax ($0.875 ea.)	_____
Los Angeles County Residents 0.5% Sales Tax ($0.07 ea.)	_____
$3.00 Shipping & Handling per order	3.00
TOTAL ENCLOSED (Round up to nearest penny)	_____

Mail to KARLIN'S KITCHEN, 1343 Sunset Avenue, Santa Monica, California 90405